PAULO VIEIRA, PhD

THE POWER OF ACTION

Make Your Ideal Life Come True

Translation
Laura Folgueira

Director
Rosely Boschini

Publishing Manager
Rosângela de Araujo Pinheiro Barbosa

Production Control
Fábio Esteves

Graphic Project
Balão Editorial

Proofreading
Carolina Cândido

Febracis
Gabriela Alencar
Lucíola Limaverde

Illustrations
Fábio Albuquerque de Menezes

Cover
Miriam Lerner

Cover Image
bubaone/iStockphotos

Printing
B&W printed

Copyright © 2019 by Paulo Vieira
All rights reserved.
Original title: O poder da ação
Rua Natingui, 379 – Vila Madalena
São Paulo-SP – CEP: 05443-000
Telefone: (11) 3670-2500
Site: www.editoragente.com.br
E-mail: gente@editoragente.com.br

Cataloging-in-Publication Data (CIP)
Angélica Ilacqua CRB-8/7057

Vieira, Paulo
  The power of action: make your ideal life come true / Paulo Vieira. -- São Paulo: Editora Gente, 2019.

ISBN: 978-65-5544-335-6
Original title: O poder da ação

1. Careers - Management 2. Careers - Development 3. Business planning 4. Marketing - Management 5. Job vacancies 6. Success in business I. Title

19-1145   CDD 650.14

Indexes for Systematic Catalog

1. Career management

I dedicate this book to Daniel, who was sent by God into my life.

For four years, his arrival was announced by people who, looking into my eyes, said I would father another child. Everyone who did so said my baby would be a boy that would bring light, joy and happiness to this world; they said he would renew the lives of everyone around him.

Daniel, my belated child. As I write these pages, my beloved wife is about to give birth.

Júlia, Mateus, your mother and I are waiting for you. Welcome, Daniel!

CONTENTS

FOREWORD	8
PRESENTATION	11
INTRODUCTION	13
CHAPTER I: WAKE UP	**20**
Waking Up to an Abundant Life	23
Anything Other than Abundance is Dysfunction	23
Abundant Lifestyle	26
Differentiating What is Normal from What is Common	29
Do I Need to Change Something in Me?	35
CHAPTER II: ACT	**36**
Tales and Stories	41
Classifying and Changing Tales	47
Exercise: Identifying and Eliminating Tales	48
Power Comes with Action, More Power Comes with the Right Action at the Right Speed	51
CHAPTER III: BECOME ACCOUNTABLE	**59**
Exercise 1	61
Exercise 2	65
Real-Life Cases	70
Law #1: Do Not Criticize People	75
Law #2: Do Not Complain about Circumstances	76
Law #3: Do Not Place Blame	78
Law #4: Do Not Play the Victim	79
Law #5: Do Not Justify Your Mistakes	81
Law #6: Do Not Judge People	83
How to Use the Six Laws of Self-Accountability	84
If Only I Had the Opportunity…	85

You Build Opportunity, You Don't Wait for It	87
Changing My Existence without Changing People	89
Confronting Yourself and Others with the Truth	91
Term of Commitment	92

CHAPTER IV: FOCUS — 93

Where to Place My Focus	94
What Distracts You from Your Focus	95
Common Distracting Factors	97
Focus on an Excellence Routine	100
Happiness Is Earned Monday through Friday	102
Multiple Focus	107
Case Study	110
1st Stage: Visionary Focus	111
2nd Stage: Behavioral Focus	112
3rd Stage: Consistent Focus	113
When Dreams Don't Come True	114
Focal-Temporal Intelligence	115
Past	115
Present	116
Future	117
Depression Model	118
Anxiety Model	120
Success Model	121
Past Model	123
Future Model	124
Present Model	125
10/90 Rule	126

CHAPTER V: COMMUNICATE — 130

Verbal Communication	132
A New Linguistic Pattern	137
Linguistic Style	142

Gratitude	143
What Keeps You from Being Completely Grateful	146
Attention	148
The Perfect Language	152
Fundamentals of the Perfect Language	155
Communication of Light or Darkness	159
When Love Doesn't Work	161
The Losada Ratio	162
Powerful Wisdom Questions	165
Non-Verbal Communication	166
Emotional Addictions	173
Eliminating Emotional Addictions	176
First Pattern: Power	179
Second Pattern: Victory	180
Third Pattern: Happiness	181
Fourth Pattern: Joy and Enthusiasm	184
Fifth Pattern: Peace	184
Sixth Pattern: Love	185
How to Practice the Patterns	187
Necessity	187
Intensity	188
Repetition	188
About Stress	188
CHAPTER VI: QUESTION	**190**
Qualifying the Questions	192
Powerful Wisdom Questions	197
Exercise	201
Self-Coaching	201
Stages of Self-Coaching	202
CHAPTER VII: BELIEVE	**204**
Reality versus Imagination	211

Beliefs as a Thermostat	212
Self-esteem	214
Belief in Being or Identity Belief	215
Opposites Attract. Do They?	217
Belief in Doing or Ability Belief	218
Belief in Having or Merit Belief	219
Childhood Beliefs: How to Build and Rebuild Them	221
ACE Quiz	224
The Beginning of Change	227
Powerful Wisdom Questions	231
FINAL MESSAGE	**234**
REFERENCES	**236**

FOREWORD

The ability to make the right decisions, to believe in your potential, and to work hard until you achieve your goals is what defines your life. A few years ago, while I was working as a doctor for the Brazilian delegation in an international competition, a yachtswoman interrupted my breakfast saying: "Doctor, have you seen the wind today?"

I saw the tension and anguish in her face, and answered:
"No, I haven't."
Then, almost in an outburst, she said:
"It's terrible!"
I realized where she was going and quickly asked:
"Is it terrible only on your route?"
She smiled and replied:
"No, it's terrible for everyone!"
"There is no such thing as terrible wind for a yachtswoman, for the wind is the same for all athletes. The ones who decide the quality of the wind are the people competing. Someone is going to win today's race and, please, let it be you. We're all rooting for you!" I added.

She smiled and left, a little calmer. The winds of life blow for everyone and it is up to each of us to know how to use them. The wind is bad for those who are always afraid, but those who have the courage to advance will always be ahead.

In moments like that, the excuse for insecurity is *crisis* (and it doesn't matter when you're reading this text, there is surely a crisis in the world and in your life). People are too worried, and I'm not only talking about drastic moments, but about daily life. Even in joyous occasions, they are concerned.

The world is taken over by fear. It seems that being scared is the new lifestyle. Insecurity kills the joy to live, because fear is joy's worst enemy. Every life change requires a new attitude that should be fed by trust, for loving with fear is dangerous. Working with worry opens the door to failure, and, most of all, living afraid is to die while keeping the body alive. Trust is the best vaccine against insecurity and worries.

The people we admire are those who achieve their life goals. On the other hand, those who left their dreams in a world of illusions are frustrated. A champion is someone who transforms the impossible into reality. Currently in your life, you probably have goals in your world of dreams. To accomplish them, you need to believe in your potential and have a method to achieve success in a much easier way.

This book solves these two challenges: it helps you believe in your capacity for accomplishment and offers you a method to enjoy success. Those who don't long to be anything will amount to nothing. They will be an abortion of their dreams. Never change your dreams. If you have to change something in your life, change your job, change your boss, change your business, but don't change your dream. Fight for it. Nobody who advises you to live with less than you deserve can be called a friend. Always believe in your dreams and pay the price for that. There is no free dream. Pay the price and celebrate it!

Ambitious people make mankind evolve. It's the scientists who don't accept the fact that a disease can end lives who find the cure for patients. Parents who believe in their children's futures and stimulate them to complete their studies.

For centuries, our society has criticized ambitious people, perceiving in them the seeds of richness. They were mistaken for greedy people, who wanted success no matter what. Ambition and greed can, sometimes, look very much alike, but their essence is completely different. The first stems from a will to accomplish something, and the second, from the desire for power.

Your achievements are the greatest gift you can give to humanity, because your riches will generate more riches for everyone. Let your generosity create opportunities for everyone to be happier.

I believe that successful people share a secret: they help others, solve problems, motivate, find solutions for other people's obstacles, and, thus, transform lives and the world.

That is why Paulo Vieira is not only a dear friend, but a professional I admire a lot. From my first contact with his work, I saw how dedicated he is to developing people, and how committed he is to his students. He is passionate about making great revolutions happen in their lives, touching the existence of those who experience his trainings, watch his videos, attend his lectures and read his books.

A work like Paulo's profoundly changes society, showing people that change is possible and teaching them with unwavering confidence in the results they can obtain. This book goes in the same direction of his work of over twenty years: to make the champion inside people become a reality. Like he says, "power comes from action." This work is an invitation for all of us to act now.

Lack of trust is a big Achilles heel in people's success. Often, it is the only obstacle standing between a normal person and a champion.

In every moment of your life, trust God, trust others, and, most of all, trust yourself.

All the best,
Roberto Shinyashiki
M.D., speaker, and writer.

PRESENTATION

The book The Power of Action presents a broad scientific investigation, resulting from Paulo Vieira's dedication during his Ph.D. program in Coaching at Florida Christian University (FCU). A good part of this material was thought and conceived at FCU, where Paulo defended his dissertation and became a Doctor of Philosophy in Coaching (Ph.D.).

In this book, the author shares achievements and learnings from his Ph.D. years, and also his path as Master Trainer Coach and creator of the Integral Systemic Coaching (CIS) Method®. He also relies on the experience acquired along over ten thousand hours of individual coaching sessions.

As president and chancellor of FCU, I have the pleasure of presenting this work to you, reader, while also taking the opportunity to present FCU. Founded in 1985, it is a global outreach higher education institution headquartered in Orlando, Florida, United States. Our mission is to provide higher education in a practical and accessible way to professionals, preparing them to accomplish their callings with Christian foundations.

FCU is recognized as an advanced member of the Florida Council of Private Colleges, Inc. (FCPC) and certified by the Council of Private Colleges of America, Inc. (CPCA), agencies that represent colleges, universities and their members with the American government and Florida's Commission for Independent Education.

About the book you have in your hands, its seven chapters present concepts and tools that can operate changes in every pillar of your life. This material will help you achieve your biggest, best potential. In the first chapter, you will be led to a deep self-analysis—Powerful Wisdom Questions raised within it will bring you to a transformation. In the second chapter, you will understand the importance of not only acting, but assertively acting to leave your comfort zone for good.

In the third chapter, the theme is self-accountability. In the words of my friend Paulo Vieira: "You are the only one responsible for the life you've been living, and so, only you can change your circumstances." You will understand that you alone can lead your paths, your trajectory, your life. However, for changes to come about, you must have focus! So, in the next chapter, the author shows that producing power and generating changes depend on concentrating on one single thing: discovering where to place your focus.

In the chapter called "Communicate", you will be presented with techniques to reprogram your beliefs and build a new lifestyle. We communicate through words, thoughts, and actions; therefore, a lot of attention is required to communicate the best in us. The way we do that directly influences the reality around us.

However, communicating is not enough; you must also question. For that reason, in the sixth chapter of this book Paulo Vieira defends that we should always question ourselves and the reality around us. The final chapter shows that changes happen quickly, that is why you need to believe and dedicate yourself to turning your plans into actions.

The main message in this publication is that we must be accountable for our lives, accept the challenges to wisely use our God-given free-will, and carry on. The whole world changes when you change first and keep on with your changes. Achievements are waiting for you.

Florida Christian University is sure that *The Power of Action* is a very rich continued education tool for students, professionals, managers, and technicians. The knowledge to which you have access here will contribute for your improvement, your development, and your growth in all areas of life.

Happy reading!

Professor Anthony Portigliatti, Ph.D.
Presidente e Chanceler
Florida Christian University

INTRODUCTION

For almost twenty years, I have dedicated my life to finding ways to help people make their dreams and goals come true and overcome their impediments and their limitations. This has been an obsession for me, in studying, reading, researching, modelling successful people and companies etc. My personal and professional background is an expression of that. I have the pleasure of being the creator of the Integral Systemic Coaching Method and the CIS® Method seminar (the Portuguese acronym stands for Integral Systemic Coaching), the largest Emotional Intelligence training in America. I have taught workshops for more than 250,000 people in four continents. I am also founder of the Brazilian Federation of Integral Systemic Coaching (Febracis, in the Portuguese acronym), one of the three largest coaching institutions in the world, with a team of over 100 direct collaborators and an international headquarter in Orlando, USA.

As a professional coach, I have conducted over 10,000 coaching hours, promoting results that, in most cases, are beyond extraordinary. My team and I have created enough technical content that the concepts and tools of Integral Systemic Coaching (Integral Systemic Coaching) are now the basis for the world's first bachelor's, master's, and PhD degrees in coaching at Florida Christian University, Orlando, USA, a Febracis partner, where I am also a lecturer.

With all that I have been experiencing in the world of coaching and human development, I can state that there is a winner in you. You have been conceived for victory and created for success. There are enough resources in you to accomplish a lot more than all the goals you have ever dreamed of putting together. Believe me, you have the capacity to make the world better and leave a positive mark for future generations.

In this book I present seven principles full of concepts, techniques, and applicable tools that will help you achieve your greater, better potential. Why not be more, do more, and have more?

It doesn't matter how your life is right now. It can be better, much better. In the almost twenty years of my career, I have been witnessing extraordinary changes and accomplishments by regular people, like in the three following cases. I hope they serve as motivation for you to continue this reading, for it will certainly change your life.

Ana Maria's Testimony
My name is Ana Maria. I did the CIS® Method seminar two years ago and started to read, study, rethink and reflect when following the scheduled agenda presented in the seminar.[1] By the time I got there, I couldn't see what was happening to me; it was like I was numbed. I was 44 pounds overweight, and I am writing this testimony looking at a picture from the time I started the Seminar... I thought I was beautiful and I lived as if everything was fine, but the truth is I was self-sabotaging all the time, and though I said to myself that I was beautiful, I couldn't walk in front of a mirror. After all, it was just one more reality I didn't want to see. After the CIS® Method Seminar, however, it all changed, and I made some adjustments to my life.

I learned there that change was possible, especially because I had a lifestyle which I though was wonderful: getting home tired, sitting on the couch, having a cold beer, relaxing... And I relaxed on Fridays, Saturdays, Sundays. Then, I started relaxing on Mondays. I had only a couple of beers and said: "That's nothing, it doesn't matter," before resting and going to sleep. Then, I started having three beers, four beers, up to five beers, and my relationships at home got worse and worse.

There were no more mother and children relationship, no more men and wife relationship, and things got really complicated. They said it wasn't good, that my way of living wasn't working, but I just couldn't see it at all. I was blind. However after the CIS® Method, a lot of realizations came immediately, while others took time. I read Paulo Vieira's books, saw all those new possibilities we learn here. My

---

[1] Scheduled agenda: a tool in which the person gets an agenda with movies, books, exercises, and so on to help establish and solidify new habits, with the goal of generating an excellence routine.

mom always told me that, if you want to lose weight, you have to keep repeating your goals: "I weigh 130 pounds in the divine law and order." And I joked that it wasn't enough: "Yeah, but if I keep eating and drinking, it won't work."

Till one day I went to visit a couple of long-time friends, and someone took a picture of our group. Upon seeing it, my blindfold dropped, and I finally perceived myself. I saw the truth, my truth. This was August 26th, 2013, and that's when I decided I would change my life. Everyone needs an incentive to do that, right? I had already promised time and time again to leave the beer and lose weight by saying: "I am going to lose weight," "I am going quit drinking" and it didn't happen. That August 26th, though, I stood in front of my husband and the couple we had visited and declared: "Starting tomorrow, my life will change." "I doubt it, I don't believe it. Let's bet?" My husband challenged me, so, I answered: "Yes, let's." They proposed 50 reais per kilo, and I said: "50 reais isn't enough, I bet you 100 reais per kilo." They replied: "Ok, we're in."

So, starting from there, my life started to change. I went to see an endocrinologist that my husband already used to see and, during the first appointment, she told me: "You will die either of cirrhosis or of cardiac problems caused by obesity. We are going straight to bariatric surgery." I told the doctor that I didn't want the surgery because it was too invasive, I didn't want to risk it because I knew my children still needed me so much. She replied: "At your age, you won't be able to lose the necessary weight, you need the surgery." However, I had a fixed idea that I could lose weight by changing my diet habits. This is what I did: I lost almost 22 pounds on my own, which impressed the doctor. And it wasn't with medication, but with a new diet that I was only able to adopt because of the changes and learnings within myself.

I started with the first thing that was ruining my life: the beer. I cut that, as well as any type of alcohol. I chose and selected foods that were good for me. Like Paulo Vieira says in the course: I woke up to myself and to life. And today, one year later, I went from that situation to something extraordinary. Seventy-seven pounds lost with no surgery or harmful medications; 77 pounds less, and I am still working on it. To sum up, I lost 77 pounds, stopped drinking, became a mom who is super-present and participant in my children's lives, and, today, I am the wife my husband wanted by his side. Not to mention I am happier, more joyful, communicative, hopeful. Now I have the confidence of knowing there are still lots of things to change in my life. Very soon I will be back at the CIS® Method, this time to talk to those who are starting to wake up, about the dreams I will accomplish this year. I am thankful, of course, to my husband, my children, and my special sponsor, professor Saraiva, who is my mentor, my coach, and my friend, and who brought me to CIS® Method.

So, thank you very much, and believe me: anything is possible, especially changes.

Vânia Barroso's Testimony
I had never heard of Paulo Vieira, and thought I was only going to another Emotional Intelligence course. It was my husband who invited me to join the CIS® Method. Actually, he is used to taking several courses, and is almost a graduated coach. Feeling despondent, I said I wasn't going, by he pushed me because the course was already paid for. Still, I insisted that he went alone. That was when he explained to me that it started early in the morning and went right into the night, throughout the weekend. Being very jealous, I found that schedule strange and decided to go with him. It was only jealousy that led me to the CIS® Method.

When the course started, I couldn't think of anything else. I lived that moment. A lot of realizations came on the first day. My husband felt the same way. On the second day, I understood even better the change proposed there. When Paulo Vieira talked about family and children, I realized I wasn't a good mother.

I remembered it was a shock taking my daughter to the pediatrician, being questioned about the medication she was taking and having to ask the nanny, who knew more about my daughter than I did! In a very cynical, but serious way, the doctor asked which one of us was the mother. That was a terrible blow.

At that time, I hadn't followed the CIS® Method yet. Only during the course did I start to do some soul-searching. At Team Coaching Life, I made the decision to dismiss the nanny, but I did so with love in my words. While I let her go, we hugged each other and cried together. What I felt was gratitude for her life-long service, but, from that moment on I decided to be everything for my children, like she had been for so many years. It was a very hard goodbye, but she understood I needed to be in the role of a mother, which was very new to me.

Waking up early, looking at the schedule, preparing their backpacks. All of this was new to me. On the first day I packed up my daughter's backpack, I forgot to put in her school uniform. It was embarrassing when I got to the school and the teacher told me that. I apologized. It was a humiliating moment, but, at the same time, a victorious day. It was my first day as a mom.

Today, I own a gelato shop which, in less than five months, has been featured in Veja magazine as the best in the city. Lines go around the corner from Thursday on. Nobody ever imagined I would be working with my husband, but, today, he is my partner. Our business is a success, not only because of the gelato itself and the lines, but because of what the customers say about the company. I have heard people comment that it isn't only the ice cream, but something else that makes them feel good. I believe our mission is to bring luck to everyone. Paulo Vieira uses the sentence "That's a Lucky charm!" in every course, as a good-humored catchphrase. And in my gelato shop, our attendants, who have also joined the CIS® Method, say the same: "That will bring you good luck." Here, we deliver the ice cream with love and believing that "It brings luck to everyone!"

I apply this to my life, and it has been very "lucky."

I did all the exercises and was truly committed, and it was definitely worth it. It was because of the post-course agenda, the movies and the books I had access to during the training that I decided to be the mother I am today: present in my children's lives. I also became a completely different wife. Jealousy? The word doesn't exist in my vocabulary anymore.

I always tell people that God uses angels, and He used Paulo Vieira in mine and my family's lives. I am very grateful.

Maximiliano Roriz's Testimony

Since I decided to change, I could see great revolutions in my life. A long time ago, I tried but couldn't, and now I can! My accomplishments happened. Criticism was heavier. Today, it is lighter. I think positively. I don't compare myself to others anymore. I know what I can do, and I pay the price to achieve my dreams and my goals.

I want to share with you, reader, the gains in my life after the CIS® Method.

A little over a year ago, a friend whose family had joined the course, invited me to CIS®. I never believed in that kind of training, but I went, although I felt a little suspicious.

On the first day, I was still skittish about things. Everything was very odd and I felt uncomfortable. But as time passed, it touched me. The realizations came.

On Friday, I went home thinking about everything I had seen and heard. On Saturday, I liked it a lot more. On Sunday, the realizations really came. I was impressed by the number of people there who had evolved using the Method. They were all sharing their accomplishments with everyone. I was also impressed by Paulo's passion. I marveled at his dedication, at the fact that he made it strong, powerful. Like he says: the CIS® is tremendous!

Right before I started the CIS® Method, I had gone to a nutritionist and decided to start a diet. I was sedentary, had back pain and other problems related to obesity. At the time, I weighed 246 pounds, now I weigh 200. I lost 46 pounds in three months!

During the course, I started to exercise, something I hadn't done in quite a long time. I didn't use to be able to run at all, and today I run four to five miles. Every day! Nowadays, I wake up early with the greatest will to run. I am determined to reach the goals that I defined in my health pillar. I am very happy for that. People see me and are impressed with my results.

In the professional pillar, a few days ago, I managed to open my own business with my brother. It has been a success; clients are loving it. Though the beginning was very tiring and demanded hard work, I no longer complain about employees. I behave as a winner towards the clients.

And as for my contribution to society, I was finally able to put in practice the goal of helping a charity institution. For a long time, I talked about it with my girlfriend, and we always put it off. Late last year, however, on December 25th, we made our first donation, and we keep making donations every month.

I also grew closer to my friends and family. I could approach them with no demands, no criticism. I don't demand love and attention. I give the affection and the love each person needs. This attitude has greatly improved my relationships with others.

Before the CIS® Method, I didn't believe in myself anymore, didn't think I was capable of getting what I wanted and dreamed of. I had a lot of bad internal dialogues.

Each day, I feel more capable, stronger. I wake up every day saying I want more. I am sure I will achieve my goals because I am focused on them. I will conquer each one of them in its own time, for I am determined. I still have a lot to accomplish.

At the beginning of this book, I bring the stories of three people who were impacted by the method presented in these pages, because I strongly believe in what is here. Living with thousands of cases of accomplishments and life transformation like these has been a wonderful reality in my life for all these years. And it is precisely because of these people, with their successful cases and this whole world of changes, that I wrote this book for you. That's right, this book is for you. And it is not by chance that you have it now in your hands. There is a reason why, a powerful and divine force that wants more for you and your life. And I believe this is your *breaking point*, a moment of moving forward to a new, higher standard of living. A moment of unparalleled realizations and accomplishments. Enjoy this book and this moment we call the present. Something grand will finally happen. What's more, something grand is already happening.

Finally, I ask you not to see this reading merely as a rational, explanatory one, but as a practical manual for high performance and great accomplishments. Here, besides deep, modern, and scientifically-backed content, you will find lots of exercises, questionnaires, and tests. And, to have the best, greatest results, I ask that you underline and highlight everything you find necessary, but, above all, that you dedicate yourself in doing and answering each of the exercises proposed. I wish you a great reading and big changes.

CHAPTER I
WAKE UP

Whoever wants to achieve their goals needs to start with a deep analysis, for their transformation process will demand firmness of thoughts and goals. We can only achieve this kind of conviction by defining, very clearly and every single day what makes us happy and what brings us down. The first step is to propose some questions, so, stop now and be honest with yourself: what has been your attitude towards life? How have you been presenting yourself to your family and other people in general, to challenges and opportunities? How do the people who know you best define your attitude towards life? Honestly, how do you present yourself to the world: with autonomy or hiding from it? "Going all in" or searching for an excuse not to go ahead? Honestly, how do you see yourself when it comes to your attitude and autonomy in life?

Watch yourself throughout the past week or month and answer in all honesty. Did you go to the gym and take control of your health or, once again, postponed it for the next Monday or next month? When you look at the shape of your body, do you feel pleasure or shame? Pride or sadness? Or do you pretend you don't even care? Have you been a reference at the company where you work, generating great results, performing tremendously, and, thus, leading your career and your professional success? Or are you just one more person filling a seat and complaining about the boss and the company? Do you keep studying and learning as a young apprentice, thirsty for more information and knowledge, or do you believe you have learned all you needed to get the best out of life and barely read one book a year, leaving your destiny adrift? At home, are you a present parent who dedicates quality time to your children and conducts your family to an abundant life? Do you seat on the floor with them, play and laugh? Or does your royal throne in front of the TV, your smartphone, keep you from being a parent capable of raising real champions?

Based on these questions, check how you really perceive yourself today in the context of the autonomy of being, doing, and having the best:

( ) as the captain in the boat of your life *or*
( ) as a sailor waiting for orders?

( ) as the director of the movie about your life *or*
( ) as a supporting actor waiting for your turn to enter?

( ) as the author of the book about your life *or*
( ) as a character waiting for his part in the next chapter?

What did these questions generate within you? How do you feel after answering them and evaluating yourself? What realizations did you have? Are you giving your best? Are you using your time to build an extraordinary life?

Not to sound redundant, but in order to search for a more profound meaning to your changes and achievements, I ask that you answer the Powerful Questions of Wisdom below in your own handwriting:

What has been your attitude towards life?
_____

How have you been positioning yourself, in terms of autonomy and action, in the realms of:
Family: _____
Career: _____
Difficulties and threats:_____
Opportunities: _____

Honestly, from 0 to 10, how much do you feel in control of the boat of your life?
_____

Are the results you have been harvesting in your life in accordance with what you want for yourself?
_____

And how much of those results are due to your lack of autonomy?
_____

The approach is very simple; each one of us have the life we deserve. Change your attitude and you will change your life and your results. Believe me, I have seen thousands of people change their attitudes towards life. People who decided to pay the price of making a change. People who decided to believe they could be, do, and have more in life.

I invite you to wake up and own your true identity, and I assure you this book will help you find it. Come on this trip to bring about a new attitude, untethered from the results you got in the past, as well as from the self-image that generated them. What matters now is the possibility to wake up the sleeping giant inside you. So, come on: WAKE UP. Wake up to live your best life today, wake up to be happy now, wake up to achieve your most important goals, and the least important, too—they are yours, after all.

I invite you to take the helm in the boat of your life and shout loudly: "Cast off, time to set sail!" I advise you to strongly clap the clapperboard and say to everyone in and out of the movie set: "Lights, camera, action…" And how about, with firm, decisive fingers, you type the next chapter in the book of your life? Come on, wake up this powerful sleeping giant in you and come with me on this journey of achievements and accomplishments.

WAKING UP TO AN ABUNDANT LIFE

ANYTHING OTHER THAN ABUNDANCE IS DYSFUNCTION

There is a biblical passage that makes me feel very good, producing in me a gigantic belief in possibilities. In it, Jesus Christ says: "… but I have come so that they may have life and have it in abundance" (John 10:10). Personally, I believe entirely in the literal truth of this passage. I believe you and I are here to have and live the best in this world here and now.

Like Jesus also says: "In this world you will have tribulation" (John 16:33), and it is true, we will have setbacks, falls, and problems during our lives. This has nothing to do with social class, race or gender: difficulties are there for every human being. However, I still believe that even the worse tribulations can and must produce learning and more abundance in our existence. In its theoretical, philosophical, instrumental, and practical basis, CIS® looks to produce abundance in every area of life. It states that everything that is not abundance is dysfunction. And it works obstinately to eliminate or diminish every dysfunction in people's lives. The catchphrase we all use at CIS® says:

> "… I have come so that they may have life and have it in abundance…"
> (Jesus Christ – Jo 10:10)
>
> *And everything that is not abundance in your life is dysfunction. And every dysfunction must and deserves to be treated.*
> (Paulo Vieira)

My great friend and master, doctor Anthony Portigliatti, told me a story about this abundant view of life.

Once upon a time an old man was fishing in his little boat. The first fish he catches is a big peacock bass. He looks at the fish, analyses it, and sends it back into the river. Right after, he catches a cachama that is over 22 pounds. Again, he looks at the fish, measures its size, and sends it back into the river. The third fish he catches is a small tilapia. He looks at it with satisfaction, analyses it, and puts it in his basket inside the boat. He returns to fishing and soon catches another big fish, sending it back into the river. And once again he catches a small fish and puts it in the basket. Seeing that and understanding nothing, another fisherman approaches and asks the old man: "Hey, buddy, I don't get it. When you catch a big fish, you put it back in the river and when you catch a small fish, you put it in the basket to take home. Shouldn't it be the other way around?" And the fisherman answers: "You know what? The frying pan at my house is very small, and these big fishes don't fit."

I have seen a lot of people dormant to their own potential, living below their possibilities. They are like the old man who throws the big fish back into the river. How about increasing the size of your pan and desiring more from yourself and your life? How about going to the market right now to buy a bigger pan and then catching the most flavorful fish in the river?

You should be clear about what *abundance* is. Does abundance mean being short of money? Is it not having money to save, to invest or to help others at the end of the month? Of course not. These situations are what we call dysfunction.

Having a body that is neither beautiful nor ugly, for instance, is not abundance. Abundance is having a healthy, strong body despite your age, a body that gives you pleasure and helps you reach your goals, a body that celebrates this, the biggest gift you have ever gotten.

People with a small frying pan believe paying the bills, even when no money is left at the end, is already a victory, when, in fact, victory is paying the bills and having money left to help others. That is abundance. How comfortable and selfish it is to have money to pay your bills when you could be helping so many people around you!

I need to firmly tell you something, reader: neither you nor I are here to have an average life. You may read these words and think: "Oh, but I don't have any problems at home…". We are not discussing problems, but the need for abundant love, affection, proximity, and respect.

You say everything is well with the people in your household, but how will it be possible to help them if you don't have enough capital? How will you help those you love if you don't have the financial means to do it? After all, you're not lacking for money, but you also don't have it in excess.

Again, it is not about shortage. The desire not to have a shortage doesn't mean abundance. What I wish for you is not only to have enough money, but to have money in excess. I wish for you to have an abundant life.

I don't want to know if you're getting just "enough," I want to know your life is abundant. I don't want to know if there are arguments in your marriage; what's important is that your marriage is abundant. If our destiny is to have an abundant life, and anything other than abundance is dysfunction, please, make your frying pan larger and catch bigger and more tasteful fish.

How about thinking about life now in terms of abundance and possibilities? And why not to have that amazing house? How about turning the activity of rolling in the grass with your children into something ordinary? Why not? And how about having your children kiss you and you kiss them every day, without the need for a special day for that? How about having abundant health to run, jump, climb? How about walking and running a few miles a day at 50, 60, 70, 80, 90 years old?

Once while travelling I was boarding a plane at the priority line with my very young children, and two older men were by my side. One of them was strong, haughty, clearly muscular, with a straight posture.

The other was notoriously overweight, arched shoulders, tired frown, and walked with some difficulty. When the flight attendant announced our entrance, the muscular man said: "Please, young men, go ahead." I found it odd that he addressed me and the older man, both as young, and I asked: "Excuse me, sir, how old are you?" And he answered, with a smile, that he was 85 years old. There was only one thing for me to say: "Wow, really? You're 85 and in such shape. Congratulations!"

After I boarded the plane, the other man in line sat beside me and said, with an air of envy or hurt pride: "Did you see that conceited old man in the boarding line? He only said that to show off." I couldn't help but ask him: "And how old are *you*?" He answered, a bit embarrassed, that he was 63. Thus, that haughty strong man had every right to call us young, after all, he was 22 years older than first guy and 45 years older than me, but in the most perfect shape.

Still in line, that super healthy man had explained to me the secret to his health. He told me he had had a heart attack at the age of 40 and almost died. That made him wake up to his life, and since then he started to eat rigorously right, to work out every day, to swim twice a week, and to walk with a group of young friends (all between theirs forties or fifties) twice a week.

Is what I am saying a utopia? Is what I am saying impossible? Is what I am saying unattainable for someone? Note that I am not talking about a life with no tribulations or problems. We *will* have problems. We *will* have difficulties. So, why not learn with every rain how to build a better roof for our houses? Why not learn with every storm how to build a stronger boat? And this is the point of this chapter. Look in the mirror and ask yourself: Why not?

ABUNDANT LIFESTYLE

Now, you might ask me: "What is an abundant lifestyle?" Imagine you wake up early, work out, make love in the morning with the man or woman of your life, play with your child, take him (or her) to school. You go to work, you love your job and what you do. And that is why you do that with pleasure, you do it well, you are recognized, and you make more than enough money to survive. You say goodbye to your colleagues and already miss them. You go for a run, see your family, and meet your friends for dinner at a nice restaurant. Then you go home, love your children, are loved by your husband or wife, get a good night's sleep, wake up the next day and shout: Yes!

That is not too much to ask, and I am not talking about a selfish life. I included your children, your wife or husband in this context; it's you, making these people happy and working for their happiness. A lifestyle in which everything is abundant: money, love, happiness, peace. When did we stop believing in that? An emotionally healthy child, for example, acts with abundance in all their plays, representing this with happy dolls, full of babies, who are also happy. Their house is colorful and full of friends, and they cook delicious things on their stove. When did something so natural in our childhood became so distant and utopic that we actually started to accept so little out of our lives?

The answer for our detachment from an abundant life perspective becomes clear when we watch TV, traditional media, soap operas, news casts, most movies, and most people's conversations. We listen to their tone and realize that the central themes covered are death, pain, fear, loss, treason, sadness, lies, revenge, hate, violence, greed, envy, inversion of values, and so on. All this information and all these stimuli come from many directions, but especially from the media. And the media we are talking about not only comes charged with high cognitive precision in what it wishes to communicate, but packed with strong, impactful emotional content which deeply targets at humans in both cerebral hemispheres: the left (cognitive one), and the right (emotional one). Through incessant repetition, our brain starts to believe that all these pieces of informational trash are the components of a normal life. Thus, we numb ourselves with so much bad information, and receive all that material in a way that is less and less critically, questioning less and finding it more "normal." To sum up: our brain, which can't resist repetitive stimuli without being changed, starts to believe that all of that is in fact real, acceptable, and, in the end, normal.

I remember a story about a picture taken at Vermelha Beach, in Rio de Janeiro, where a couple of tourists took a selfie with the Sugarloaf Mountain at the back and a corpse by their side. The amazing thing was how normal they acted posing next to a dead body so as not to miss the best scenic angle. Very clearly, death had become something normal for that couple, not to say trivial. A human being drowned, a life ended precociously, a family without one of its members, a mother without a child, and (probably) children without a father. And still no awkwardness, no shock, a life seen as banal and unimportant. There are so many stories about murders, kidnappings, death, violence, catastrophes, wars, etc., that all of it becomes ordinary. So ordinary that we unconsciously put a label of "normality" in all this information that keeps coming.

The same thing is true of poverty in Brazil: it is so common that is has become "normal." Crowded buses and trains carrying people piled up, huddled together, pressed against one another: this is also completely "normal" in Brazil today. I can't count the number of people I talked to, trying to show them none of it is normal. I can't count the number of times I said: Wake up! You, me and Brazil deserve a lot better than that.

And I will leave up to you to identify another bunch of values and concepts that traditional media has pushed down our throats as normal. Once again, people exposed to these stimuli start to live well below their possibilities and their potential, as if numb by a superpowerful anesthetic called mediocrity. Why so much acceptance? Why do we take things that are so important and vulgarize them?

To close off this explanation, neuroscience proves that our brains end up accepting and even searching for the pattern we repeat the most. When our minds, looking for safety and subsistence, compare our lives to news casts, soap operas, news stories, movies, and everything that surrounds us, they start to believe that the average events which have been so ordinarily presented are in fact normal, acceptable, and even desirable. So, after so many impactful stimuli, we have brains that are programmed to search and produce "normal," known lives just like the models to which we were exposed. All that is left is to live mediocre lives with no questioning and no great expectations. Lives below our real potential possibilities.

DIFFERENTIATING WHAT IS NORMAL FROM WHAT IS COMMON

In order to illustrate this matter, imagine the following scenario of a "normal" life.

A father, already contaminated by these negative stimuli communicated by the world around him gets home exhausted, tired, stressed after ten hours at work. Passing by the living room, one of his children, who is listening to music, waves to him with only a slight raise of the eyebrows, and nothing more. At that moment, an internal voice (called the voice of consciousness) questions this father, saying: "Is that how your child welcomes you after a full day of work?" And the father immediately answers the voice in a mocking tone: "Young people, young people. They're like that. They all live in their own world. That's **normal**." After passing by his son, he goes towards his room and sees his daughter, who is paying attention to her phone and doesn't greet him. Again, the voice interrupts his path and asks: "How about your daughter, who is not so young anymore, won't she greet you with a word or a hug?" And again, he answers: "That's the way children are. They all in their own world. That's **normal**." Then, in the hallway, he finally makes conversation with someone. His wife, not looking at him or demonstrating any enthusiasm, asks: "Did you bring bread?" This time, the voice is stronger and more inquisitive: "Your own wife won't get up to welcome you after a day of work?" And, with a ready answer, he says: "After twenty years of marriage, do you think wives greet their husbands at the door with a kiss, saying 'I love you?' That's life. It's **normal**."

After passing by his whole family, he takes a shower. Getting out of the bathroom, he goes to the kitchen, gets his plate from the oven, sits alone at the table and starts what would be a silent meal, if not for the noise of cars coming through the window. Again, the voice says: "Are you going to eat alone? Your whole family is home and you're going to eat alone?" Once again, he answers: "Each one has their own life, their own things to do. You know how it is. That's families nowadays. It's **normal**."

When he finishes the dinner, he sits at the living room table and starts sorting through the bills he will pay and the bills he won't be able to. The voice reappears, this time sounding inquisitive: "Are you not going to pay all the bills this month?" And again, with a prefabricated answer, he interrupts the voice, saying: "With the life we lead today, not paying one bill or another in time is **normal**!"

However, this father's journey at his house doesn't stop there. After sorting through the bills he will pay and those he won't, he goes to his room, lies on the bed, turns the TV on and watches an action movie just to relax, while his wife is glued to a social network. Now in despair, the voice questions him: "Aren't you going to talk to your wife about your day, caress her or make love?" And the man answers to the voice that had been questioning his whole life: "Don't you realize that we have been married for twenty years and things are just like that? Everyone lives like this! For the hundredth time: this is **normal**! My wife likes social networks and I like action movies, and that's it."

After an hour, the action movie has turned into a porn film, his wife is asleep and even though he is exhausted, he doesn't feel sleepy. He tries to sleep, but can't. He turns off the TV and keeps his eyes open. Not being able to relax, the alternative is to take a "sleeping pill." He swallows one, but there's no effect. After the second, the voice, already tired of its owner and his lifestyle, asks once again: "Are you really going to take two sleeping pills?" And also tired of having his life confronted by this voice (which doesn't let up), he answers with a heavy heart: "Who doesn't take a sleeping pill? Nowadays, everyone takes them. That's **normal**." Then, one hour after the second pill, sleep comes – a superficial one, with heavy breathing, and a scary sleep apnea.

The cellphone beeps, indicating it's 6:30 in the morning. He wakes up still tired and late for work. He leaves in a hurry without saying goodbye to his wife and children. Inclement, the voice asks: "You aren't going to leave without saying goodbye to your wife and children, are you?" To which he replies resentfully: "Don't you see I'm late? I don't have time for this. In this busy world, no one has time for that nonsense. That's how it is, it's **normal**."

And before getting into work, he has already gotten involved in two fights in traffic, not to mention the obscene gestures made to another driver who cut in front of him. Now, the voice is silent, not asking or questioning, just letting him go about his everyday business. The voice of consciousness is silent, won over. And, in its place, comes a new one. A voice that jokes about his own disgrace. A negative, ironic, justifying voice. When he gets to work, stressed and angry, he stops at the door, sighs, takes a deep breath, and walks in with his head low. He comes in without talking to anyone, without looking at anyone, without saying hello to his colleagues, and goes straight to his office. After all, he was going to spend the next ten hours doing something he didn't want to do, with people he wouldn't like to be around, and getting paid a lot less than he thinks he deserves. And before the voice of consciousness could bring him to his harsh reality in an attempt to wake him up to life's possibilities, comes the pessimistic, negative voice of common sense. Ironically, it says: "This is **normal**. Who likes their job? That's life. You have to put up with this annoying job while nothing better comes along. Family to provide for and bills to pay. That's **normal**." Now, it was a negative, pessimistic voice talking. And all it did was say that it was all **normal**.

At the end of the work day and beginning of the night, this man gets into his car, faces the same traffic jams, and gets home. Standing there by the door, he looks down, takes a deep breath, and enters. As if he's watching the same DVD, the movie repeats once more. One more day that man is living his own sad routine. A man who isn't actually living, but surviving his own life, acting a lot more like a supporting actor than the author of his own life. And, thus, accepting whatever part is available.

Do you know anyone who, in one way or another, has a life that is similar to the character above? Do you know someone who lives such a precarious life and might not even realize it? Do you know anyone whose voice of consciousness talks, yells, alerts, advises, and begs for change to the point of being silenced? One thing is obvious and I can guarantee it: NONE OF THAT IS NORMAL. We can't mistake what is normal for what is common. Talking coldly to one's wife might be common, but it isn't normal. Taking sleeping pills might be common, but it isn't normal. Not having a conversation in your house might be common in many homes, but it isn't, in anyway, normal. Being overweight is common, but it isn't normal. People are confusing and substituting what is common for what is normal.

Don't get carried away by the world around you and what it communicates. Don't believe limitation is normal. Don't believe loneliness is normal. Don't believe sadness is normal. All of that can be common and ordinary in the lives of a lot of people who allow themselves, by action or omission, to fall into the comfort zone of the pseudo-normal. However, for you, reading this book, none of it is normal. Remember: "… **but I have come so that they may have life and have it in abundance," and anything other than abundance in your life is dysfunction. And every dysfunction must and deserves to be treated.**

Other people's life experiences and results belong to them. They are neither your experience nor your reality. Your results are up to you. Just because a lot of people live a certain way, that doesn't mean you should. You own your life and should live it according to what you believe is best for you, not to what seems common to other people. I will narrate the case I just described again, but in an unusual way which maybe few people experience. And then you will understand what I really want to explain about what a normal life really is.

A man comes home from work and, entering his home, his youngest son runs to meet him at the door, hugs him, leans his head on his chest, kisses his face, and says with a genuine interest: "Hi, daaaad." With a hug and a kiss, he asks how the boy's day was. Believe me: this father-son relationship is what is normal. The father barely takes five steps before his daughter puts aside her phone and, very affectionately and sweetly hugs and kisses her father, walking him to the living room. When he gets there, he is greeted by his wife with a passionate kiss and a tender hug; with her eyes, she says how much she loves him. Once again, all of *that* is normal. I will say it once more: that is a normal life. Anything different than that is abnormal, dysfunctional, and mediocre. After taking a shower, he sits at the kitchen table accompanied by his wife and children. His dinner is a special moment of familial conversation and love around the table, not the TV. That is a normal family. After dinner, he sits with his wife by the living room table and, together, they plan next month's budget and see that, this month, there was also a good amount leftover, which they will use to invest and achieve the family's dreams. Believe me, that is possible, and it is a normal financial life. After finishing the month's budget, the whole family sits at the table to play, chat, talk, and maybe watch a movie that is actually worth it. This is definitely not very common for most parents and children. However it is truly normal. As I have said, anything less than that is abnormal, dysfunctional, and mediocre.

After this family time, comes bed time. The father goes to each child's bedroom, cuddles them, has a brief private talk, blesses their sleep, and says good night. He gets back to his room and finds his wife. They talk, share their day, talk about their doubts, their plans, their accomplishments, their afflictions, their joys. Right then and there, without being distracted by a TV or a smartphone, they express love in the way they look at one another, caress one another, and might even express that love with sex. The fact is, they love each other. That is a normal married life. It doesn't matter if they have been married for three years, seven years, fifteen years or fifty years. This is definitely normal in a married life.

He sleeps early with a sense of fulfilment, wholeness, knowing that his life is worth living. The next day, he wakes up early, thinks about his future plans and dreams, exercises, and then enjoys a healthy breakfast with most of his family. He goes to work feeling enthusiastic and joyful. How marvelously normal that is! He arrives at the company and gets in triumphantly. He greets each one of his colleagues with smiling eyes, sincere smile, and optimistic words. He is polite and supportive, beloved, respected, recognized by everyone as an expert in what he does. This man feels great pleasure in working and producing. When his workday is over, he is filled with a nice sensation of a job well done, a super productive day. And, before leaving, he says goodbye to his colleagues and leaves with a smile on his face, eager to get home, knowing there are people waiting for him in the coziness of his house. That is in fact normal. When he gets home, it all happens again, in different ways, but with the same emotional quality, the same feelings. That is a life well lived, a truly normal life, not ordinary at all.

Regardless of the situation your life is now, the first thing to do to change is WAKE UP and understand the difference between normal and common. Then you need to know that it is possible to have a wonderfully normal life. And, last but not least, be willing to build a life pattern based on a routine of excellence.

During my events, it is very common to have people asking my team if I in fact live what I preach. Is my family like that? Is my relationship with my children filled with love, affection, warmth, respect? Are my wife and I indeed a happy, loving couple? The answer is a clear, loud yes. We *are* happy, we *do* have a dynamic, passionate life. Are there challenges along the way? The answer is also yes. However, even in challenges we grow, get better, and become even happier.

Now that you know there is a great difference between a normal life and a common, ordinary life, I invite you again to WAKE UP. Hear the voice inside you, hear the voice of God, and don't accept anything less than a truly abundant life. Come on, jump out of bed and come to a normal, uncommon, wonderful life, available to everyone who is truly willing to build it.

DO I NEED TO CHANGE SOMETHING IN ME?

A lot of people use to say that happiness is something very unique, for it is defined differently by everyone. I don't agree with that idea. I believe people have diverse ways of having fun and everyone searches for their way of feeling joy. Joy, however, is not only fleeting, but not our focus. Here I am talking about an abundant lifestyle, about perennial, real, existential happiness. And I understand that, to be truly happy, we need to enhance each area of our lives. After all, a high-level job in a company can't, by itself, make anyone happy. Having lots of money and not having a harmonious family doesn't really do much in the context of happiness.

So, be alert. Your life is not what you say it is, but what is perceived, seen, and experienced in reality. You can't just say you are a good father and your children are happy if you don't dedicate time, quality time, to them. You can't just say you are a good father if your children aren't emotionally strong, vigorous, and happy. So, it doesn't matter what you or I say, it doesn't matter how we see things; sometimes, even our certainties about day-to-day life don't matter. What matters are our behaviors and, especially, the results generated and perceived by all.

Do you want to know if you are financially successful? Then remember it is not what you say or show people that determines your financial stance. What determines if you are successful is how much money you made over the past year. What confirms if you are financially prosperous or not is how much money there is in your financial applications and real estate.

Do you want to know how you have been as a spouse? Look at your marriage, look at how many times your husband or wife kisses you, look at the respect you have for each other, look at how you fall asleep and wake up. How many times have you looked into each other's eyes? How many times do you hold each other during the day?

Be honest and brave to look at your life and see how it has really been. Evaluate it with a very open mind. And, if it is not abundant, it is time to wake up and start acting.

CHAPTER II
ACT

How long will you lie there, you sluggard? When will you get up from your sleep? A little sleep, a little slumber, a little folding of the hands to rest—and poverty will come on you like a thief, and scarcity like an armed man.
(Proverbs 6:9-11)

Picture a big wooden cask, like a giant wooden barrel. It is 10-feet tall and 6.5-feet wide, made of dark wood with metal strings around it. Unlike a common cask, this one doesn't have a lid on top; it is always open. Come on, I would like you to picture this cask with all its details. It doesn't matter if you are not good at drawing, what matters is that your brain represents this image internally. Don't think of this, however, as unnecessary child play, since it is actually a very important stage called Internal Metaphorical Representation, or IMR. After all, the comprehension of the external world happens inside of us first. And big changes or realizations come about in the way we represent internally the reality around us. Can you think of any character in history who, with the stories and parables told thousands of years ago, changed the world we live in today?

Here, you can see the big wooden cask.

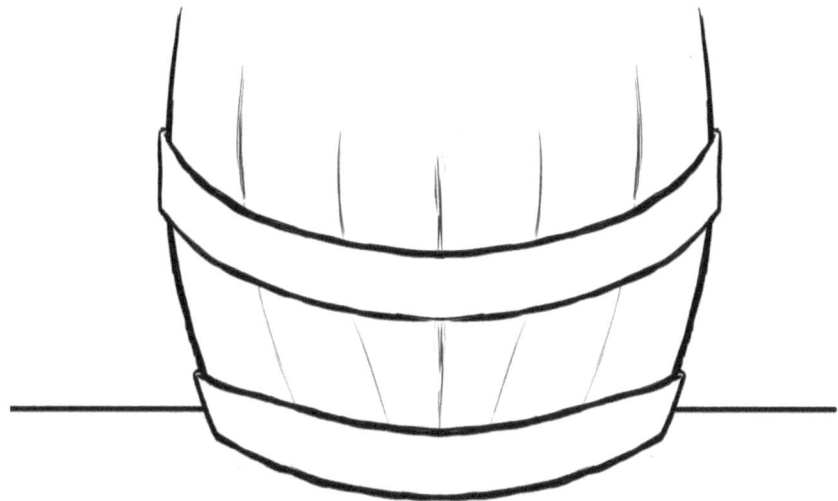

Okay. Now you have the cask's drawing. Feel free to put more details in the image, as I give more characteristics and information.

To add to this representation, I ask that you see this cask as full, overflowing with a foul, malodorous substance. A dark brown, gooey, doughy substance. Lots of flies and insects fly around and, in the cask, and also around the gooey substance. Remember, the smell is insufferable, to the point that it drives away most people in the area. Draw this other series of details that complement the cask's image.

Then, suddenly, you see a dear person inside the cask, leaning on the edge. The person is dirty, fetid, and exposed to all the rottenness inside it. Worried and anguished, you yell at the person: "Get out of there. Please, get down. This is very, very bad for you. Come off." You keep going: "Time is passing, and nothing will change for the better while you're standing there, come on!" You don't stop: "Face life, have courage. Standing there won't do you any good. There's no use denying it. Those who know you know your fear, your paralysis, your omission towards life. Move, dare to get out of there, come here. If it doesn't work, you can start over... Come, please, come down."

And the person you love so dearly stays there, not moving. Sometimes accusing you, sometimes justifying things, sometimes silent. You might be having a dialogue with another person on top of the cask: "Come here. Get down from there... Alcohol is killing you. Please, stop and look at your family, your parents, your kids. They know you're an alcoholic. They all know. They don't tell you, but they know, they talk about it... Stop it, come down here. You reek of alcohol. You're losing people's respect, and their admiration you lost long ago." You don't give up on that person: "Come down from there, they don't deserve that from you. Come here. You deserve more from life. We are here for you, get off the booze, come... As long as you're up there, we can't help you. Look at your children, they deserve better from you. Clean yourself up, come here. This is your place, come."

Or the dialogue with that person could be like this: "Get out of there. This is not your place. You can do more, much more than that. Come down. Come take responsibility for your financial and professional future. Stop pretending you're doing things. Stop pretending you're trying. No one believes your excuses anymore. Do something and stop being a burden for others. They don't deserve it. Get out of there and come work and be productive for real, come make money. Get down and build your financial and professional independence. No matter your excuses or disguises as a successful person, everyone knows where you are and who you've been. Please, stop disappointing people, take a decisive stand, and do something, get down from there..."

During my professional journey as a coach, I have seen many people who wanted to help their family and friends to get down from the big cask. They used every means and every strategy. I once heard a friend say something like: "Friend, get out of there. Come down. People are talking about your extramarital affair. Come down before your wife and children find out. They don't deserve that from you. Look at your daughter, look at your son. Look at your faithful, dedicated wife who has always supported you. Stop it before it's too late. Friend, you stink of sex and everyone can smell it. Please, do this for you and your family, come here. Let me help you clean up. Come on. This cask isn't the place for you."

Another time, I heard a brother say to his sister: "Sister, get out of there. Please, come down. People realize and talk about how remiss you have been with your children. Your children are suffering, abandoned. You're soiling everything around you with your lifestyle. Stop spending money on clothes and purses. Stop going to so many concerts, parties, travels. Stay home with your children; they need you and you need them even more. Get out of there, come down from that cask. Staying on top of it is destroying your life. Believe it, you won't find what you are looking for in there. Your children are not to blame for the end of your marriage, come home, own your motherhood while you can, while they are children and need a mother. Come back. Come on. Get down…" In other cases, I heard worried people call out, even beg the person on the cask to get off the drugs. Others implored that the person on the cask stopped smoking. Others still supplicated that they would eat less and exercise before another stroke.

The fact is that all the people I mentioned, for one reason or another, were in their comfort zone. In our metaphor, the comfort zone is represented by the people standing on the cask, but, really, the comfort zone is a place where we find excuses not to do what we know we should. The comfort zone seems like a supposedly safe place, but, in practice, it chains us and keeps us locked up, stagnant, immobile while the world is happening out there, and we are growing old up here. A great definition of comfort zone is that it is a mix of expired paralyzing lies. The comfort of not doing the right thing at the right time will soon become a prison with high walls.

Comfort zone is a mix of expired paralyzing lies.
(Paulo Vieira)

After all, we don't need to be paranormal or clairvoyant to imagine the fate of that person who never took on a professional life. We don't need to be very clever to know what the alcoholic's future will be, or that of the adulterer's family. Or what will happen to the sedentary glutton's health, or to the life of the woman who has replaced her children with party acquaintances and her financial future with purses and shoes. It is certainly a lot easier and convenient to predict people's lives in their comfort zone. After all, we are on the outside looking in, analyzing their actions and the consequences of their omissions. We need, however, to look inside us and ask ourselves:

In what areas of my life do I see myself in a comfort zone?
_____
_____
_____

What will my life be like if I stay, by action or omission, in the comfort zone?
_____
_____

If you understand the cask metaphor for what a comfort zone really is, as well as its consequences in people's lives, but especially in yours, I can then extend a second invitation to you: ACT. Come on, leave the cask. Come here and get away from that terrible comfort zone. Act. Right or wrong, it doesn't matter. Just act. And then, apply yourself to act more, and more wisely.

There is a catchphrase that says: "Power comes with action; more power comes with the right action at the right speed." I ask that you commit to mind this phrase I have been repeating for the past years, and then share it with others.

Power comes with action; more power comes with the right action at the right speed.
(Paulo Vieira)

The one thing that can push someone off their comfort zone is directed action. Directed towards your goals, your objectives, and your desires. But pay attention: to take you off the comfort zone, it is not necessary to put in practice the wisest action, nor the most effective. Any action subtly directed towards your goals will initiate the process of change and liberation from the comfort zone. However, there is a pachydermic force that sustains and keeps people imprisoned in it. And our focus right now is to identify, qualify, and, then, destroy it. When that happens, you will find yourself soaring and ready to land on your most important goals, miles and miles away from what you used to call your comfort zone. Let's get to that force.

TALES AND STORIES

I believe, as I have said before, that we were created by God to have an abundant life in all aspects. I also believe that the events in anyone's life should, by themselves, lead them to this pattern of excellence. It is like a river's waters flowing towards the sea. That is the nature of a river. To stop it, it would require a great effort of building barrages or deviating the natural course of the water. Abundance is God's nature and, consequently, human nature. If, however, you are not living that abundance and fullness, it is because there is a barrage, a deviation that keeps this nature from flowing towards you. And, oddly enough, we are the ones who, through our behaviors—sometimes "innocent and unpretentious"—create real barrages and deviations for all the good that is supposed to come our way. In reality, if we just got out of the way, good things would come. The good news I bring is that besides not getting in the way, we can also use this gigantic force to speed up the flow of good things in our lives. We will call that force *"tales."*

Tales are linguistic, verbal, and mental structures that validate, explain, and justify our failures, our flaws, and our lack of success; a sometimes subtle and sometimes explicit way of not being responsible for results, actions, and behaviors that didn't work in our lives. How comfortable and less onerous it is to be fired and have a whole rehearsed *tale* to explain or justify what happened. How easier and more comfortable it is to face the school headmaster when your child has just been expelled and tell the *tale* of how you raised both your children equally and only one is problematic. Apparently tales bring comfort, but, in reality, they have two devastating consequences in people's lives. First, they attack self-accountability (a concept that will be better explained in Chapter 3), meaning they take away their author's autonomy, making them hostage to the situation. In the case of a father in front of the headmaster, the tale puts him as an impotent victim, as if he couldn't help it. After all, his other child never had problems at school, and they were both raised the same. The second consequence is that this tale is interpreted as true by the brain. The more times it is told, and the more emotional intensity is put into saying it, the more a person is stuck in it. The brain doesn't choose what to believe, so whatever you communicate most is the truest. In this case, the child will really become the family's bad apple, the problem child, probably with no solution. How many tales have we told to justify our failures? How many tales have we created and told to justify or explain our permanence in the great comfort zone hotel?

It is common to believe that tales are little lies or simple disguises for something from which we want to run or about which we don't want to acknowledge our responsibility. In truth, there are three categories of tales: lies and exaggerations; truths; and, finally, jokes. Deceitful tales are justifications made up with the goal of diminishing guilt. True tales are an attempt to accuse others and exempt yourself from responsibility for your own actions. Jokes make people close their eyes to the problem, draw focus away from the subject through an anecdote or something funny said about the problem. Whatever the type of tale, it destroys their self-image and leave their authors impotent to act and behave, and certain of their impossibility to achieve things.

To better understand the tales, let's use three real examples:

Case 1

Once I met an old commercial partner. We started talking and eventually got to the subject of health. At that moment, he looked gravely at me, with impotence, and confided: "You know, I don't eat anything and still can't stop gaining weight." His wife, who was with him, looked down and gave a tentative, ironic smile. He continued: "My doctor says my metabolism is too slow to burn fat, and that's why I'm so overweight." With respect and firmness, I asked: "What tests did your doctor do to evaluate your metabolism and how many calories you burn?" And my ex-partner's wife answered: "That's a tale, Paulo Vieira, all talk. He doesn't even have a doctor. The problem is he eats too much junk food, especially at night, before bed. Our bed looks more like his picnic table, and the TV is the landscape."

In this first tale, as denounced by the wife herself, all the husband's talk was a lie. First, he did eat a lot, especially at night. Second, no doctor told him his metabolism was too slow in burning calories. It was just an lie to explain his obesity, taking away his responsibility for the extra pounds. And since the obesity problem wasn't his responsibility—the slow metabolism was responsible—, why change? Why adopt a healthy lifestyle, since your metabolism burns calories in the speed of an aquarium turtle?

Here is how we can classify that tale:
- Category: lie.
- Behavior: justification and diminishing guilt for being obese.
- Primary result: obesity.
- Possible secondary results: health problems, marital problems, low professional productivity, low sex drive etc.

Case 2

I was talking to a businessman who was in trouble. He opened up and told me the reason behind all his financial difficulties. He said this in a tone of victimization and impotence: "This country can break anyone. One day the dollar is up, the next day it's down. I imported some things because the dollar was down, and now it is up by 40%. How am I going to pay it? I am taking out loans at incredibly high interest rates. Not to mention I have products that are being held at the ports for over two months. And the worst part is the turtle-slow operation speed of our supervisory body. That's how it is in Brazil, everything is difficult for businessmen."

What he said is, indeed, true. The country has no clear rules, and worse, these rules can change overnight. Besides that, there's a lot of bureaucracy, and completely inefficient mechanisms and government structures. Not to mention the alarming levels of corruption and so on. However, if that was the only problem with his company, why would his competitor, who actually started long after him and with no capital, be doing so well and growing tremendously despite the government and the so-called "Brazil cost?"[1]

Unlike the previous example, in this case the tale is true: all the accusations towards the Brazilian government are valid. However, when we examine the businessman's sector, we see companies thriving despite all the country's economic problems. Why is he not prospering? What are his successful competitors doing that he is not? Knowing both him and his company, I can say three things with conviction: first, he is very centralizing and doesn't allow anyone to act or think about solutions without him. Second, his leadership is autocratic and very strict; he commonly loses it and offends his team. And last, as I have told him, he lacks corporate management. But why change all that, starting with himself, if the problem is government inefficiency?

Let's classify this tale:
- Category: truth.
- Behavior: accusation and attempt to exempt himself from responsibility for his financial crisis.
- Primary result: business crises.
- Possible secondary results: financial troubles, emotional troubles, difficulties in relationships, health problems due to stress etc.

Case 3

The third example is a talk I witnessed among two professors during a common friend's book launch. One of them looked at the other, who

---
[1] Brazil cost: All the internal expenditures and characteristics that burden production and investments in the country, such as road condition, corruption, taxes, energy etc.

had an athletic gait even at 55, and said jokingly: "You're looking well, eh, Alberto?!" The friend answered: "Thanks, Carlos, I've been putting a lot of effort into it." Carlos, who was overweight, did not miss a beat or the joke, and completed laughingly: "My huge belly is actually a sexual callus from making so much love." They both laughed, and the conversation went on another direction.

Whenever we joke about something, we keep it from gaining too much importance, making it light and unimportant in our minds. That's ok. The problem is when the issue is relevant and calls for massive, clear action. Our brain doesn't distinguish what is real from what is an innocent joke. Every time that man repeats the sexual callus joke, his brain believes his disproportionate belly really is unimportant and doesn't do any harm. Thus, there is no intellectual or emotional mobilization in searching for a change of habits or behaviors. The true story is that, more than just his being overweight, that teacher's disproportionate belly was due to the fact that he drank copious amounts of beer and, unlike what his joke claimed, had nothing to do with too many nights of sex.

Let's classify that tale.
- Category: joke.
- Behavior: closing the eyes to the problem, diminishing its importance, and drawing focus away from the issue.
- Primary result: misshapen body.
- Possible secondary results: health problems, financial problems, difficulties in love life, low self-esteem, feelings of inferiority etc.

In over 15 years of coaching and classifying the state of each of my clients by their behaviors, it became evident to me that tales were the cornerstone of their incapacity to change habits, attitudes, and even results. I realized empirically, but in a very consistent way, that even the simplest behavioral changes were stopped by the telling of these tales. In other words, telling these tales made my clients incapable of promoting any kind of change towards their goal. By observing that, I started to follow a path in the change process both for my individual coaching clients and for the

CIS® Method. And I got lots of changes, each one deeper and faster. But how can change happen? Easy: by exchanging tales for stories. Stories are simply true narratives that make you responsible for the actions that generate consequences in your life. It is not enough for the story to be true; it needs to make you understand that you are the only owner of your trajectory and that your actions are the ones that create results. Thus, it is up to you to change what isn't working to get to a desired goal, sometimes much needed and urgent. So, don't tell tales. Even if they are true, you must understand they are not beneficial in the least. You shouldn't repeat them lightly, either, believing this will have no practical negative effect in your life.

Let's move forward and understand the change process through tales and stories.

1st step: Identifying in which areas of your life you are getting poor results.

2nd step: Identifying what those poor results are.

3rd step: Identifying, for each unwanted negative result, what tale or tales you have been telling to justify, explain, or not be accountable.

4th step: Identifying each tale's classification (category, linguistic behavior, primary result, and secondary result):

Categories: a) deceitful tale; b) joking tale; or c) true tale that doesn't need to be told, but overcome.

Linguistic behavior: a) give a real explanation; b) justifying what happened; c) exempting yourself from responsibility for the result; d) closing your eyes to the problem; e) drawing focus away from the unwanted issue; or f) others.

Primary result: Negative impacts that this tale actually produces in the life of the person telling it.

Secondary results: What negative impacts have been happening or could happen because of the primary results?

5th step: Tell a new story. This is the last stage of the change process. This new story should be based on desirable behaviors and results we want to achieve. In other words, you need to create a (self-fulfilling) prophecy that brings not only new results, but new behaviors.

Let's use the three examples given before to exemplify the fifth step. My ex-business partner who wouldn't stop gaining weight should stop telling the destructive tale that he didn't eat a lot and got fat because of his slow-burning metabolism, and start saying something prophetic, like: "I am strong, healthy, and thin. I feed myself with excellence and I eat what is best, at the right time, and enough to feel healthy and well."

For the businessman with problems in his company, the new story should be something like this: "Regardless of the government, my company is prosperous, lucrative, and growing. I have the best team and my leadership is incredibly effective. We plan and execute with primacy. My company is number 1 in its segment and I am recognized by my style of corporate management."

The teacher needed to change his whole approach about his health. Instead of frequently repeating the joke, he should at least be quiet and not undermine the importance of something serious, since his belly could represent a lot in terms of self-esteem, marriage, and health.

Now that you understand what tales are and what results they produce, I ask that you dedicate yourself to filling out the whole questionnaire below, so that, as well as cognitive comprehension, you have real, palpable change in your life. Follow the model and the examples given to fill the whole classification and substitution of the tales. To reinforce: do not go ahead without doing the proposed exercise before. If necessary, repeat this exercise for each negative area and the destructive tales that cause the problems.

CLASSIFYING AND CHANGING TALES

Tale 1:_____
Category: ( ) Truth   ( ) Lie   ( ) Joke
Behavior: _____
Primary result: _____
Possible secondary results: _____

Tale 2: _____
Category: ( ) Truth   ( ) Lie   ( ) Joke
Behavior: _____
Primary result: _____
Possible secondary results: _____

Tale 3: _____
Category: ( ) Truth   ( ) Lie   ( ) Joke
Behavior: _____
Primary result: _____
Possible secondary results: _____

EXERCISE: IDENTIFYING AND ELIMINATING TALES

Step 1: Identify which area of your life is deficient.
_____
_____

Step 2: Identify the negative results you have been getting in this area.
_____
_____

Step 3: Identify the tales you have been telling about that area that have been producing negative results.
_____
_____

Step 4: Identify each tale's classification (category, linguistic behavior, primary result, and secondary results):
Category: _____
Linguistic behavior: _____
Primary result: _____
Possible secondary results: _____

Step 5: Create new, restoring stories to substitute the tales.
_____
_____
_____

Just out of caution, I ask that you answer all the questions below that have something to do with what you are currently living.

What tales do you tell about the success you still haven't achieved?
_____
_____
_____

What tales do you tell to justify your financial troubles or the fact that you still haven't achieved your financial goals and dreams?
_____
_____

What tales do you tell to continue being rude or impatient with your kids?
_____
_____

What tales do you tell to keep drinking, smoking or using drugs?
_____
_____

What tales do you tell yourself and others to explain being obese or unfit?
_____
_____

What tales do you tell yourself and your spouse to justify the lack of sex in your relationship and/or the lack of harmony?
_____
_____
_____

What tales do you tell yourself to justify being out of the house for so much time, with friends or working?
_____
_____

What tales do you tell to explain the fact that you are not working in what you should and could?
_____
_____
_____

What tales do you tell yourself to spend so much money with futile, superfluous things?
_____
_____
_____

What stories do you tell to explain why you are having troubles in your company or your career?
_____
_____
_____

Now that you have answered these Powerful Wisdom Questions (PWQ), it will be easier to execute the whole strategy. You know what area of your life is not working, and also what tales are leading you to these negative results, and keeping you there. Your biggest challenge, however, starts now.

First, you need to understand and be serious about the impact of these tales in your life, so that when you inevitably start repeating your past tales, recognize all the harm they cause in your life. Second, whenever you speak or repeat these tales, you should have your new story at hand, and repeat it emphatically at least five times. Last, this new, prophetic story should be repeated aloud five times a day, until, by repetition, it became true in your behaviors and results.

POWER COMES WITH ACTION, MORE POWER COMES WITH THE RIGHT ACTION AT THE RIGHT SPEED

I have already invited you to act. It does not matter if you do it completely right, for acting is the first step to achieve your dreams and goals. And now, without the tales that kept you from acting and acting wisely, it will be easier to use all the power of action that exists inside you.

A lot of people believe that what separates them from their goals is the size of their objectives and the place where they are at the moment. That's why we frequently see these people setting narrow-minded, small, mediocre, and lots of times insignificant goals. After all, they say: "If I establish a goal that is too daring, it will take a long time to achieve it, or it may never happen." This affirmation seems true, but, in reality, it isn't. Humanly speaking, the only thing that separates us from our goals is our ability to act. The quality and sum of our actions are the factors that will determine how long we will take to achieve a goal. It doesn't matter if your goal is daring or very easy to accomplish. I constantly see people who take an eternity to achieve a simple, small objective, and I have seen others who do the extraordinary in record time. What will truly matter is what you really do to achieve your goal, that is, the quantity and quality of actions implemented.

Let's use the example of two young salesmen in a wholesale company who decide to establish their personal goals. The first one decides to buy a simple economy car. The second one establishes the goal of buying a brand-new Mercedes. The first salesman uses the traditional Cartesian logic and starts doing the math: if I save U$ 50,00 a month, I will need 36 months or three years to get U$ 1,800 for the down payment in my economy car, and I can pay the other U$ 16,200 in 72 monthly installments of approximately U$ 225,00.

To sum up: the first salesman will need five years for a down payment in his economy car, and six more years to finish paying it, totaling 11 years. This salesman with a logic, Cartesian thinking established one single action to accomplish his goal: to pay small, almost infinite installments. The second salesman, however, thought the following: first, I will dedicate myself and work ultra-focused, to beat all my sales goals and win all the prizes in the sales campaigns. I will also take two courses in sales and sales management, and study the manuals of the products we sell, so I have more knowledge about them and more arguments when it's time to sell. This first stage will take four months and double my current income. With that, I hope to be promoted to coordinator of the commercial team, earning two times my current salary. The second step will be to get into a technical college and graduate in two years. As soon as I complete my undergraduate studies, I will get into a graduate course in commercial management. This stage will take two years, and then I will apply to be a commercial manager in the new unit the company is building in a nearby town. At that time, I will already be making, in fixed salary and commissions, approximately four to six times more than my original wage. My next step will be to propose to the company's directors that I build an outsourced telemarketing team to take care of the company's small sales, when it isn't financially worthy to send a route salesman. After all, that is today the company's biggest bottleneck. With that, I will be able to assemble a telesales team in four states, which will save the company a lot of money in sales costs, route, fuel, cars, etc. With the company's portfolio of small clients, the total estimate sales are R$4,000,000 a month. And, if my telemarketing company's commission is 7%, its revenue will be R$280,000, with a net profit of approximately R$80,000 a month, according to the calculations made by the management consultant who oriented me.

In the fourth month, after taking the sales courses, studying the products' manuals, and being willing to pay the price of being super-focused in selling, I will buy my car, which for the time being will be an economy car. When I am promoted to commercial coordinator in the sixth month, doubling my salary and my commissions, I could already buy a better car, but I won't. I will save and invest the money to build my telemarketing company in the future. After graduating and when I am studying commercial management, I will be promoted to general manager of the new unit, which is being built, and double my salary again. Once more, I could afford to buy a better car, but I won't. The last stage to buy my Mercedes will be to get a partnership with the company where I am a salesman today. Thus, I will own my own company and buy my dream car.

When we observe the two salesmen, we see their actions are determined by their decisions. These, however, are determined by the size of their dreams. (We saw the metaphor of the fisherman and his frying pan, and how that is decisive in people's lives and choices.) The first salesman dreamt of an economy car, while the second one dreamt of a Mercedes. The first one was content with only one kind of action: to create a small, mediocre savings account, which would never dare him to be better. The second one, looking at his daring, challenging purpose, opted for actions that would completely take him out of his comfort zone.

What is your goal? Are you sure about it? Is it what you truly want? Excellent! So, now you need to walk (act), and in the right direction (with effective actions). The faster I walk, and the more directed I am towards my goal, the faster I will achieve it. It doesn't matter if my objective is to make my first million and I don't have a cent today.

It doesn't matter if you weigh 260 pounds and want to weigh 150. What matters is whether you are going in the right direction, with the right behaviors, and at the best possible speed. I know people who started making money much later than others and, in three, five, six years were already millionaires, while the people who had started their financial journey ten or fifteen years earlier couldn't get the same result. A lot of people are talking about success, but very few are indeed acting.

In 2014 I ran my first half marathon in Rio de Janeiro. After completing the race with pleasure and physical well-being, I told my friend and trainer: "Edge, it wasn't as hard as I thought it would be. In fact, it was easy!" And he answered: "Completing the 13.1 miles in a half marathon is easy, the hard part is preparing for it." This echoed in my mind and gave me a lot of clarity about the path to success.

The hard part is acting in the right direction: waking up early for training, lifting weights, and stretching. The really hard part is to make sprints and run up hills. The hard part is waking up every Saturday at 5 a.m. and running an average of 9 miles. In reality, the hard part is preparing myself through massive, consistent actions. For success itself is only a consequence of my actions.

> *In reality, the hard part is preparing myself through massive, consistent actions. For success itself is only a consequence of my actions.* (Paulo Vieira)

If my goal was to run 13.1 miles in the marathon, to achieve it, I needed massive actions of preparation. So, I ran every Tuesday and Thursday, and Saturday I ran double the usual distance. However, it wasn't just about fulfilling the days of training. There were other questions: Did I train adequately? Did I commit to it? Did I go to my limit? Did I follow the guidance of my trainer or coach? Did I give my best? Did I eat according to what was agreed, following my diet to create lean body mass, muscle, resistance in my joints? To complete a 13.1-miles race can be easy or disastrous. It depends on your actions. The fact is that anyone can do it. I saw people in their 70s and even 80s complete the race.

My question is: are you acting in the direction of your goals, and consistently? That is the essential question for you to reach your goals.

Think about these statements:
- Making money is easy. The hard part is learning and doing the right thing to achieve that.
- Being successful is easy. The hard part is preparing for success.
- Having a sculptural, healthy body is easy. The hard part is abdicating from pleasure.
- Having happy, prosperous children is easy. The hard part is learning and being willing to educate them the right way.

I will tell you something that happened to me. In 2008 I was in bed at night reading, and my wife was updating our financial spreadsheets. With a note of disappointment, she said that we wouldn't fulfill our financial investment goal that year. And I asked her: "Why aren't we going to make it?" She answered that the year was about to end, it was already September, and we wouldn't have enough time to achieve our goal. At that moment, I said, joking, but also disagreeing with her: "Woman of little faith, the year has barely started, for we still have September, October, November, and December. In that time, we can do a lot and make a lot of money! If you can do great things in a day, imagine in four months. We will meet our saving and financial investment goals." Looking at me in disbelief, she said: "Okay, baby."

The next day, we won a car at a Father's Day raffle at a big mall: a Honda Accord worth R$120,000. Soon after, we closed big deals, opened a new area in the company, invested heavily in distance learning with a tremendous platform, and even started a coaching congress in the United States. All this happened in four months. Those who are on the outside looking for a tale to justify why they are not successful could say my success was chance or luck. But see, we didn't become the biggest coaching institution in Latin America by luck. The truth is we acted with precision, efficacy, and diligence. Attributing the growth of CIS® to luck would be denying that, in 2008, I had already conducted over 5,000 hours of coaching sessions. It would be denying that each year Febracis truly revolutionizes its innovation and management. I believe the more dedicated I am to work, the more I learn; and the more I innovate, the luckier I am.

I will tell a parable that you certainly have heard before, but that is perfectly adaptable to this theme. It even explains why I am lucky.

> *For it will be like a man who, going on a journey out of his country, called his servants and entrusted to them his property. To one he gave five talents, to another two, to another one, to each according to his ability. Then he went away.*
>
> *He who had received five talents went at once and traded them, and he made five talents more. So, also, he who had the two talents made two talents more. But he who had received the one talent went and dug in the ground and hid his master's money.*
>
> *Now, after a long time, the master of those servants came and settled accounts with them. And he who had received the five talents came forward, bringing five*

talents more, saying: "Master, you delivered to me five talents; here, I have made five talents more."

His master said to him: "Well done, good and faithful servant. You have been faithful over a little; I will set you over much. Enter into the joy of your master."

And he also who had the two talents came forward, saying: "Master, you delivered to me two talents; here, I have made two talents more."

His master said to him: "Well done, good and faithful servant. You have been faithful over a little; I will set you over much. Enter into the joy of your master."

He also who had received the one talent came forward, saying: "Master, I knew you to be a hard man, reaping where you did not sow, and gathering where you scattered no seed, so I was afraid, and I went and hid your talent in the ground. Here, you have what is yours."

But his master answered him: "You wicked and slothful servant! You knew that I reap where I have not sown and gather where I scattered no seed? Then you ought to have invested my money with the bankers, and at my coming I should have received what was my own with interest. So, take the talent from him and give it to him who has the ten talents. For to everyone who has, more will be given, and he will have abundance. But from the one who has not, even what he has will be taken away. And cast the worthless servant into the outer darkness. In that place there will be weeping and gnashing of teeth."

This passage is called The Parable of the Talents, and it is from the *Bible*, Matthew, Chapter 25.

How about you, what have you done with your gifts and talents? Have you been acting and taking advantage of them? Or have you been static, inert, and settled? Are your actions and behaviors full of dedication and effort? Or do you act haphazardly, not caring about quality or result? I know it wasn't a mere coincidence that my wife and I got the car in the raffle. It was just God compensating His dedicated, responsible, diligent servants. He gave us so much bounty because he knew we would not bury his gift, on the contrary, we would use it to create even more impact and change in many people's lives.

Don't be afraid to be overweight or with no money. You only need one fear in your life: the fear of not acting in the right direction and at the fastest possible speed. "Paulo, can I lose weight?" You can. "And how much can I lose?" I don't know, you could eat well, but if not with the necessary discipline you could lose 80 pounds or 800 grams. You could lose 50 grams a day, but also 200 grams a day, healthily.

My friend: pay the price, act in the right direction and at the fastest possible speed: marriage, children, work, money... We are talking about action. Only those who act have power. If you are obese, then plan and calculate how you will lose 150 grams a day, how much you will lose in a month, how much in six months. And when the planning is done, just act.

"But, Paulo, I don't know how!" Then get out of your comfort zone, pay the price, go search for a great nutritionist, buy the best nutrition and weight loss books, and in three or six months you will have the body of your dreams, the health of your dreams. "Paulo, I want so hard to make my first million..." Pay the price, search for guidance, the best courses on finances and reprogramming of financial beliefs, and this material will teach you the right direction to follow, and at the best possible speed.

After everything I have said, do not believe success comes just by acting. For more than thirteen years, I acted consistently, but with no wisdom or knowledge. For thirteen years of my life I had few free weekends and very little rest. I worked desperately from twelve to fourteen hours a day and achieved nothing but a precarious maintenance of my life. I wore myself down and even got sick because of the combination of intense work and no rest. So, do not believe success is only about waking up early and working hard. I have seen many people who were mistaken by this half-truth. You need to work hard and with dedication, but if your actions aren't wise and effective, you will move a lot, but never leave the same spot.

Where are the information and the knowledge that will lead you to each action and behavior that will guide you in the right direction? Search for that information! Why acting right here, and then acting wrong there? Why not getting it right much more than you get it wrong? If you need knowledge, pay the price for it. Go look for this knowledge, and it will make you walk in the right direction. Look for an emotional attitude that will make you not only go in the right direction, but do it fast, with the right posture, instead of wasting time; focused, not dispersing or distracting. I can assure you: it is worth it.

And considering that those who act have power, and those who act right have more power, think about the first five actions that will dramatically change your life for the better. Write them on the lines below.

1st _____
2nd _____
3rd _____
4th _____
5th _____

Now that your actions are correct, contextualized, directed, complementary, and sequential, I ask that you perform them, following the pattern of a conventional action plan used by many companies: the 5W2H action plan.

- What to act/do
- Why to act/do
- Where to act/do
- When to act/do
- Who will act/do
- How to act/do
- How much will it cost

In this website, you can download the tool mentioned with further explanation: www.febracis.com.br/opoderdaacao

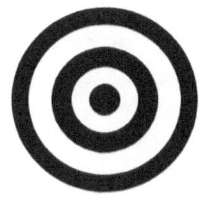

CHAPTER III
BECOME ACCOUNTABLE

You are the only one who is responsible for the life you have been living. You are where you put yourself. The life you lead is absolutely your merit, whether by your conscious or unconscious actions, by the quality of your thoughts, your behaviors, your words. As painful as that is, you are the one who got your life to where it is today. So, only you can change this circumstance.
(Paulo Vieira)

The statement above may seem too harsh, it may even seem like an accusation. However, I ask that you understand it not as such, but as a freeing reality. The belief that you are the one who put yourself where you are, or at least allowed it to happen is very healthy. After all, if you put yourself in this situation, as bad as it might be, you were the helmsman of your life, you were responsible, you were the conductor of your path to here. And, as a conductor, as a helmsman in your life, you obtained results, not necessarily failures.

From that perspective, if you are not satisfied with the results you have gotten, you can just acknowledge what is wrong, acknowledge that your choices and your paths have not been satisfactory, and then redirect them responsibly, objectively, and consciously.

Be certain that the events of your life are no coincidences, no fatalities, and that you are not a victim to anyone or to the circumstances. Self-accountability is the rational and emotional ability to hold yourself accountable for everything that happens in your life, as inexplicably as it may be, as much as it may seem to be out of your control and your hands.

How many times you saw someone in a negative, fragile situation and asked them: "How are things?" And they answered: "They're going the way God wants." If you are alert, you will notice that they are subtly taking responsibility for the negative results away from themselves and blaming God. Could God be working against people? Surely not.

Like the Bible says, however, "God cannot be mocked; a man reaps what he sows" (Galatians 6:7). These people don't realize their **behaviors**, **thoughts**, and **feelings** are creating their lives, and usually search for external explanations for their misfortunes and bad luck. So, become accountable for your actions, because they will bring consequences. Become accountable for your choices, because they will determine your paths, and these will deter-mine your fate. Become accountable for your thoughts and feelings, because good feelings and good thoughts structure our beliefs and accomplishments.

> *Self-accountability is the belief that you are the only one responsible for the life you have been leading, and so you are the only one who can change it.*

(Paulo Vieira)

EXERCISE 1
Rewrite, in your own words and in the first person, the two definitions of self-accountability present in this chapter.
Example: I am self-accountable; therefore, I am the only one...

New definition 1:
_____
_____
_____

New definition 2:
_____
_____
_____

By thinking this way, being and behaving as the author of your own story, you will be able to put yourself anywhere else, write and rewrite your paths and choices. Self-accountability portrays the fact that you have already been putting yourself wherever you are, consciously or unconsciously.

The attitude of self-accountability empowers you to change what needs to be changed in order to keep advancing towards your conscious goals and a balanced life. It is important to know that all our intentional changes and planned accomplishments start after we assimilate and start living according to the concept of self-accountability.

Like everything in life, believing it or not is a matter of choice. Believing only you are responsible for the life you lead, and that you build your life's circumstances and events, is also a matter of choice. Just the same, it is also a choice to believe that things happen totally randomly and unpredictably, that we are victims or prisoners of our own destinies and just react to the world and the events.

I myself prefer to believe we create our experiences through words, behaviors, and/or thoughts, and that everything we communicate, think, and feel generates palpable results and goals in our lives. Successful people know how to get results using not only their mental structure, but also their body language, as psychologist and Harvard researcher Amy Cuddy states.

When the results are bad, these people learn with them and responsibly opt for a correct mental structure: they start talking and thinking differently and behaving differently. After a defeat, people who have great conquests don't blame the circumstances, other people, or fate. They take responsibility for the results and ask themselves: What should I do differently for results to be better next time? One of our company's areas of expertise is professional outplacement. It is amazing to see how the absolute majority of those who seek a new position in the labor market refuse all responsibility for their unemployment. The excuses, disguised as explanations, are always the same:

- "There was a layoff in the company and I was unfortunate to be a part of it, you know how it is, I was only in the company for six months."
- "My superior felt threatened by my performance and had it out for me."
- "There is a big crisis and the staff was cut, you know…"
- "They promised me something and when I got there it was all different, so I felt unmotivated… I was fired, but I actually already wanted to quit."

Few are the ones who recognize their mistakes, showing maturity and learning possibilities. Here is how these people behave:

- "My work wasn't good, I didn't give my best, and I was fired. Today, however, I recognize my mistakes, state that I will no longer commit them, and that is why I really want this opportunity to…"
- "I wasn't humble enough to receive orders from my superior, and our relationship deteriorated until I was let go. It was, however, a great lesson, and I am ready to start again the right way."
- "There was a layoff because of the crisis and since I wasn't meeting my goals, I was fired. Starting now, I am willing to do it all differently, meet my goals, and give my loved ones reasons to be proud."

• "When I started in this company, I was looking for a job with a set time to get in and out. When I got there, however, it was insane, intense work, wherever I looked there were goals and results. I didn't want to go along with it, because I had other priorities and a different rhythm, so I was fired, and am now searching for something more akin to my goals."

The fact is that, as long as people don't recognize they were fired because of their flaws, at some point they will repeat the same mistake in their lives. In time, they will be asking themselves if someone did something against them, if it's karma or if God doesn't love them.

The inability to live in self-accountability makes us relive the same painful circumstances along our lives.
(Paulo Vieira)

If you don't believe you have free will to create and write your present and future life story, if you don't believe you are creating your world with every thought and every decision you make, if you still think your successes and failures don't depend on you, this all demonstrates that you are adrift at the sea of circumstances, living dangerously at the mercy of others and the world. For you, who believe life is a series of accidents, there is only one question left: Who is responsible for the fruits you have been reaping? Certainly someone is in charge. And, if it is God, remember that, since the Eden, He gave human beings free will. Are you the kind of person to whom circumstances and facts simply happen, and you just go along, not as a protagonist, but as a supporting actor; a puppet who later, without giving permission, is invited to laugh or cry?

Brazilian composers Bernardo Vilhena and Lobão wrote a song that, loosely translated, said something like this: *"Vida louca/ vida breve/ Se eu não posso te levar/ Quero que você me leve..."*[1] The question is: lead where? To a sad life, as the composer says later, or to happiness?

---
[1] In free translation: "Crazy life/ brief life/ If I can't lead you along/ I ask that you lead me...".

Being self-accountable is having absolute conviction; believing you are the only one responsible for the life you have been leading. Consequently, you are the only one who can change it.
(Paulo Vieira)

Thinking like this is one of the best ways to evaluate and develop your level of emotional maturity and, therefore, exponentially increase your ability to perform. It is the conviction that validates all your other strengthening beliefs. It is the guarantee that you are a person made not only of ideas, but also actions; an achieving person—alas, a person able to build a happy, bountiful life.

Psychologist and researcher Daniel Goleman and his coauthors Richard Boyatzis and Annie McKee, in the book *Primal Leadership: Unleashing the Power of Emotional* Intelligence, say that only 2% of the human population in fact produce change, 13% see changes happen, and sometimes even support and help the other 2%. And 85% of the world mass don't realize what is happening, and just follow the great herd in the direction foisted upon them.

These percentages are not about social, cultural or economic class, since this 85% is composed of very rich people and very poor people as well. We also see people from the basis of the social pyramid in those 2%, and it is incredible to see them change the world with their ideas, their work, and their vision.

My question is, where are you? Mark it below.

I am a part of the: 2% ( ) 13% ( ) 85% ( )

If you are a part of the 2% who produce change, you are a great leader. There are people around you who follow you; your words and actions make a difference in countless people's lives. You are recognized and admired by those who surround you. If you are a part of the 13% who realize and even support change, you have a leader or follow a valuable idea, relating to it. In some way, even without much effort and not exposing yourself, you contribute to a better world.

People who are a part of the 85% are manipulated and led by the system. They leave in immediate pleasure, have a narrow, short-term view. Their outlook doesn't go beyond the parties on Friday and Saturday.

These people don't see changes happening around them because, in fact, they don't recognize themselves. They don't know for sure who they are, let alone how great the value of their divine essence is.

EXERCISE 2

Write below an extraordinary vision of your life. Write about the life you have always dreamed of having. There is no limit to dream. Define what you would like to be, do, and have. Describe your most fantastic dreams, with no criticism or judgment of what is possible or impossible. Just convey your extraordinary life vision.

_____
_____
_____
_____
_____
_____

Now, compare the extraordinary life vision you just described with the life you have been living, the one you described in the previous chapter.

Be certain that circumstances are created by you and, thus, only you can change them. However, to change the circumstances, first you need to make a firm decision to break up with the past, and you also need the persistence and perseverance to keep the same vision and winning behavior, regardless of external conditions.

This is what Nelson Mandela, who spent 27 years in prison—lots of them in solitary—did. While many of his cellmates whined, putting themselves as victims of apartheid and the white colonizers, Nelson Mandela saw himself as the author of his story. He held the white minority accountable for the fact that he was in jail; however, he considered himself to be the only one responsible for his feelings, his thoughts and his attitudes in there, as well as for what he would do when he left. While seeing his cellmates succumb, he was preparing to become South Africa's first black president. He studied Public Administration, deepened his knowledge of International Law and Penal Law, as well as other important subjects for his future, all while incarcerated.

When his colleagues and even the guards saw him in such good mood and so happy, some said: "Mandela, wake up, you're in prison, and you're only leaving for your funeral." Others, in an attempt to understand so much determination and happiness, said: "How are you always so well?" To which he answered: "They may have locked up my body, but I control my mind (thoughts and feelings)."

How about you bring to your life this powerful concept from the lives of people who have achieved a lot? When events don't generate the results we expect, when our lives are not going the way we want them to, we basically have two choices: the first is to take responsibility for the results, learn from them, and change. The other one is to find someone to blame and somehow exempt ourselves from accountability, placing in others and/or in the circumstances the responsibility for what happens in our own lives.

I have been training, following, and coaching hundreds of executives and managers. More and more, I realize the difference between the prosperous and the limited; the ones who make money and the ones who just show up. The limited usually think a lot, contemplating especially what might not work, and thus become experts in justifying their flaws and explaining why things didn't go the way they planned.

They tend to be people with great ideas, but who don't carry them out. That's the type of professional who usually helps their colleagues brainstorm, shows them what they are doing wrong and what they need to do to succeed. Amazingly, they are often right, their ideas are good, and their analyses are coherent—they are, however, just ideas. And the most critical thing is: their ideas are usually only good for others. They are left only with the reasoning and explanation of why their own actions and plans don't produce valuable results.

> *A great idea that comes from deep contemplation with no action to put it into practice equals frustration.*
> (Paulo Vieira)

On the other hand, accomplishers generate good ideas. They might not be the best ideas, which might not even be their own, but they can put them into practice, or make them happen. And, if they don't get the expected results, they don't complain, and definitely don't justify it. Successful people simply assume they are where they put themselves and, humbly and wisely, try to learn from their mistakes and get better results next time.

Remember: successful people don't usually give up their dreams, they learn from their mistakes and persevere, stay focused on their goals, but do it differently the next time, by thinking, acting, and feeling differently.

Studies by scientist Jill Bolte Taylor, author of *My Stroke of Insight*: A Brain Scientist's Personal Journey, show the brain's left hemisphere is responsible for logics, memory, systematization, and reasoning. This is where our whole ability to elaborate ideas resides, as well as our abilities to plan, create, and comprehend. It's where the famous Intelligence Quotient (IQ) is located. The left hemisphere is the mathematical, classifying, exact, linear, analytical, strategist, practical, and realistic side of the brain, and is also responsible for language. The right side, in turn, is responsible for emotions, feelings, involuntary thoughts, unconsciousness, intuition, and beliefs. It is the side responsible for our ability to accomplish. This is where the now famous Emotional Quotient (EQ) or Emotional Intelligence is studied at large by famous psychologist and Harvard Ph.D. Daniel Goleman, as well as by so many other scientists and researchers around the world. The right hemisphere is the creative side, which develops art and poetry. It is the side that feels passion, longing, sadness, and it is also responsible for imagination.

Prosperous and victorious is the human being who can integrate these two areas of the brain, having great ideas and being able to put them into practice. But if I had to choose between having great ideas and contemplations or being an achiever, I would elect the right hemisphere and the ability to carry things out, even if I were carrying out mediocre ideas. It is much better to carry out mediocre ideas than to have great, spectacular ones and never put them into practice. I have seen people prosper a lot putting old, tired ideas into practice, or even appropriating ideas abandoned by their creators.

Once, I gave a speech about pedagogical excellence through CIS® for 200 teachers in a higher education organization. A Management professor, apparently very intellectually competent, disagreed firmly that she was responsible for everything she was going through, and fundamentally discarded the concept of self-accountability.

She protested: "A person's life is determined by their knowledge and contemplation of that knowledge." Next, she started talking about Karl Marx and a lot of theorists of capitalism and socialism, about Einstein, Newton, Rousseau, and other thinkers. She spoke animatedly about what we know and how we reflect upon those knowledges. In a way, she was right, or else, she was 50% right. Reflecting is indeed very important. As I have said, however, without the ability to carry out and execute my plans and ideas, I will be only left with frustration.

In a macro context, these thinkers and their theories are vitally important; however, in a personal, practical context, no theory is worth anything if we are tied up and paralyzed by reflections and thoughts, especially if those intellectual theories reinforce us as mere spectators, unable to change or rewrite our history. After she spoke with such fury, after feeling accused, I presented to everyone Albert Einstein's opinion on the matter:

> *I think 99 times and find nothing. I stop thinking, swim in silence and the truth comes to me ... We should take care not to make the intellect our God; it has, of course, powerful muscles, but no personality ... Reality is merely an illusion, albeit a very persistent*

one ... Imagination is more important than knowledge ... A person starts to live when he can live outside himself.
(Albert Einstein)

After being confronted with these ideas by Einstein, the professor who had protested me contemplated, had a series of internal dialogues and anxiously asked me to continue. Afterwards, she confided in me: "Maybe that's the path to solve my existential problems..."

When that professor spoke about how she disagreed, another tried to start a wave of applause with the other participants, going against the concept of self-accountability. It is important to mention this other professor, who also did not agree with the concept, came into the auditorium with a completely reactive attitude, didn't take part in any group dynamic, her posture and her body language demonstrating complete rejection to the institution where she worked and to that moment.

These two professors certainly weren't in control of their lives. Things weren't as they would have liked and will probably stay the same until they can become accountable for their life and their fate; until they stop placing blame for their lack of success and failures; until they stop feeling like victims. To prosper, they will need to stop hating the world as if it is their lives' villain; they will need to stop treating themselves like victims and eliminate their self-commiserating attitude.

As creator of CIS® and international lecturer, I have been to every kind of company and gotten to know many types of professionals. Those who are self-accountable are optimistic and motivated, regardless the circumstances. Even if they don't get paid as much as they want, they give their best; even if they are not that valued, they are still productive and joyful.

When circumstances become adverse and uninteresting, they opt not to complain, not to criticize, let alone to blame the company or its managers for the way they feel. They search for the solution within themselves and, if they don't find it, they simply go towards their goals, ethically excusing themselves to go their own ways and responsibly creating their stories—certainly, successful ones.

REAL-LIFE CASES

The following testimony illustrates this exact attitude of self-accountability: Carlos is now a store manager for one of the biggest shoe retailers in Brazil. His story, as told by himself, is as follows.

"I was a manager at one of the men's fashion stores of a local group. It was all going great until one day the stores' supervisor quit and was substituted by someone else in the company. As soon as he started, the new supervisor announced that all the managers who were friends with the old supervisor would be replaced. And that's what he did: little by little he fired everyone who was friends with the former supervisor, until he got to me." After a lot of persecution, Carlos was fired.

People around him were stunned by his attitude: he wasn't angry, much less looking for revenge. "If this company doesn't recognize all my hard work and my results, then this isn't my place, there must be a better place for me," he used to say. And the way to keep growing wasn't to place blame and criticize the new supervisor. Something that, to many, would be a problem, to him was an opportunity.

So, less than a month after Carlos had been fired, the supervisor in another big shoe-selling group heard about his story and his mature, impeccable posture, and hired him to manage one of his stores. "It's been ten years in this new group, and I have never been happier personally and professionally in all these years. My first store here had 12 salesmen, the current one has 90. I never stopped growing. Today, I am really valued," Carlos concludes. It was certainly his self-accountable attitude that made this achievement possible.

I always say: those who act have power. Self-accountable people are like that: they act, they don't become paralyzed thinking about injustices or failures. They know that, consciously or not, they have created those situations, whether with their behaviors, thoughts, actions, or by omission. That's why they recognize themselves as captains of their lives, they recognize that their chosen path did not generate good results, and all that is left is to opt for a new route and a new path. They act actively and live in the first person. They are eternal apprentices.

I have seen a lot of salesmen who complain about their companies, the uncompetitive prices of their products and services, the bad quality of what they sell, criticizing superiors and bosses. However, I have seen others in the same companies and teams who sell the same products and generate great results with the same conditions, the same circumstances and the same resources, but with one great difference: their attitude and the belief that they alone are responsible for the life they have been leading—thus, they are the only ones capable of changing it.

One manager told me: "For me to be a great manager, my team had to be more proactive and committed. They would fill their reports and performance reviews without the need to be reminded. The company's marketing would be more aggressive and, mainly, my director would be more comprehensive and less demanding." After the emotional intelligence seminar and a few coaching sessions, his speech changed, and, with it, his whole behavior and attitude.

He started talking and acting like this: "I know I have been lax and remiss. Most of my team is very good, but they need more follow-up and impositions. A small part of the team, however, doesn't have the attitude or the potential to be in the company, and I should have had the moral courage to replace them.

"In any case, they all need my experience and training. In fact, my director already gave me multiple chances, and I still wasn't able to take advantage of them. This time, I am not going to try or do my best, I am just going to act and do what should have been done long ago. I will take responsibility for my team's results and, if we don't get the expected results, I will know I was responsible. I am at a juncture where to keep justifying and explaining my lack of success won't help in this job or any other. It is my turn now! My career and my life are only up to me. My time has come!"

In one month, this manager proved his speech was true: with changes in his attitudes and behaviors, his whole team changed unimaginably! He was also surprised, because he didn't believe his changes had so much power, that they could generate such deep, powerful changes in the team's sales, proceedings, and organizational climate.

In another case, a salesman in a car dealership confided to me: "Everything in this company is wrong: the sales salon is old-fashioned and cramped; the brand we sell is in decline; our technical assistance is the worst in the world, it only makes the situation worse. How can you sell like that? The problem isn't me, it's the others who won't let me do my job right."

He kept going: "Paulo Vieira, the ones who need training and consulting aren't me or the sales staff, but the directors. If I could change the company, if I were the manager or the owner here, then everything would be different. But, you know, the gods send nuts to those who have no teeth… So, I live my life the way God wants it."

It was all very clear to me: it was a typical case of a salesman with no self-accountability; a salesman who felt wronged, victimized by the world, the circumstances and the company. His whole failure was caused by others, and he "unfortunately" didn't have the means to change his "poor existence."

After so much moaning and self-commiseration, I couldn't take it anymore and asked: "How long have you been in the company?" "Eight years," he answered. "So, did you go to a lot of seminars and know all there is to know about these cars and this brand?" To which he replied categorically: "I doubt anyone here knows more about this brand and sales than I do."

"So, please, answer me: Why are the rookies, young guys with not a lot of experience in cars and car sales, outselling you?" Promptly, as if he were expecting the question, he answered in an angry, victimizing tone: "If they were here from the start, they would be like me, unmotivated and tired of going against the grain."

Hiding my impatience for so much self-commiseration, I continued the coaching process: "And why are you still in this company after all this time, if you don't agree with its internal policies, strategies, and physical structures? What is keeping you from looking for something better, more compatible with your potential and style, if you are so good? Why didn't you go after a company who can recognize your value and experience?"

He stayed quiet for a while, not answering any of these questions, looked up searching for a convincing answer, then gazed to the horizon, and, at last, looked down. His physiology became humbler, and his eyes filled with tears. Then, he said: "Actually, everything is different. There used to be a lot more clients, and there weren't so many brands competing with us, it was just Ford, Fiat, Chevrolet, and Volkswagen. Now, it's crazy: Toyota, Renault, Peugeot, Honda, Mitsubishi, Nissan, there's over 30, a lot of them with factories here in Brazil, not to mention imported cars."

Nostalgically, he went on: "When the founder ran the company, it wasn't so hard on us, we had more freedom. The truth is, it was a lot easier to sell a car. Customers were willing to buy, and salesmen only needed to pay attention and take their order. Every day it gets harder, customers are more demanding, you need to put in a lot more effort into it. And, to make it worse, you people from consulting firms come with your talk of pre-sale, post-sale, prospection, performance reports, goals charts, they are even asking for sales additional. It's too much change. And I… I don't know if I can do it."

At that moment, he stopped, thought a little, and continued: "I think I'm a little in the comfort zone, maybe even addicted to the past. I'm not a child anymore, I don't know if I can comply with so many changes." Visibly emotional, for the first time he allowed himself to think sincerely about his professional life and his future. He allowed himself to think about his flaws and his shortcomings, about what he had been doing and what he should do.

Thinking of his speech, I said: "The beginning of your turning point is already here, because you were able to look inside yourself and use your self-consciousness to see what is good and what is bad, what should be kept and what can be changed. Congratulations! Your life has started to change in this instant."

To emphasize his possibilities of change, I presented him with two premises used in CIS®:

Premise 1: We all have the resources we need to prosper and be happy.
Premise 2: If anyone could, you can, too.

His semblance started to improve, he held his head higher, his shoulders projected back and a smile spread over his face. He asked: "Do you really think I can be one of the company's best salesmen?"

"Of course. If people with no experience can, just imagine you, with all your knowledge and experience. But your success depends on just one thing: That you continue and do not let go of the self-accountable attitude, recognizing that what you have been living is the result of how you have been thinking, talking, behaving, working, and facing life.

"Change yourself, and the whole world will change around you. Change yourself and you will experience a new life. This decision is only up to you. It is important, however, to know that the fruits of your change will come at the right time. It is essential to keep pursuing self-accountability and not to give up midway."

I gave this salesman my book *Eu, líder eficaz* [I, Effective Leader], and, in a very short time, I could appreciate and delight myself with the emergence of a new person, a new professional, who, after a lot of changes, was able to redirect all aspects of his life: familial, marital and social, even improving his health and physical appearance. And in subsequent talks, he told me the tool he used the most was the set of six laws to achieve self-accountability.

Six laws to achieve self-accountability:
1) If you are going to criticize someone... keep quiet.
2) If you are going to complain about the circumstances... suggest something.
3) If you are going to look for someone to blame... look for the solution.
4) I you are going to play the victim... play the winner.
5) If you are going to justify your mistakes... learn from them.
6) If you are going to judge someone... judge their attitude.

These six practices, transformed in daily habits, will bring about so many changes that not only you, but also the people around you, will realize a new person was born. New opportunities will be coming to your door and they will realize very good things are happening, apparently with no explanation, then you will see the magic of self-accountability has reached you and you will know that when self-accountability is incorporated to the way a person lives, it produces real wonders.

Let's understand better each of the laws of self-accountability, shall we?

LAW #1: DO NOT CRITICIZE PEOPLE

In English, "to criticize" means: to consider the merits and demerits of, and judge accordingly. It also means: to find fault with; point out the faults of.

Please, don't tell me your criticism is constructive and that your real goal is to help others. Never in my life have I seen someone criticize another person with the intention of helping. How do you feel when someone looks at you and, sounding like they know more than you about the subject, says: "Look, I want to make a constructive criticism, but it's for your own good!" As soon as these two words—constructive criticism—are pronounced your face drops, you look down and prepare for the "smack" to come.

If the focus and intention were in fact positive, the person wouldn't be criticizing. They would keep quiet or give an idea. Their focus would be on what was right, not on what was wrong; something that would make the listener feel up, not down. If you are one of those who love to criticize and analyze everything, and still feel that criticism is a necessary evil, try to give a suggestion or an idea instead of voicing a criticism. You will get greater results, people will want your company and guidance, something that doesn't happen with those who like to criticize.

Remember: it is very easy to criticize, it is very convenient to talk about someone else's flaws, but that keeps us from seeing ours. When we stop criticizing, our focus becomes the solution, not the problem. Our subconscious mind starts to be accountable for the events and, in a magical, unconscious way, decisions and attitudes become more in line, more proactive, more mature, and, finally, more productive.

LAW #2: DO NOT COMPLAIN ABOUT THE CIRCUMSTANCES

The definition of the word "complain" is very clear, with no margin for interpretation. To complain is to claim or express pain, displeasure, etc.; to find fault, declare annoyance; and to make an accusation. Unfortunately, there are people who base their lives on complaints and rampant demands, creating for themselves a very poor, needy existence.

In the *Bible*, there are lots of accounts about the power of words spoken by people. Despite that, lots of Christians are still verbally careless, using words of complaint and whining as a sword with no grip: the more they try to use it, the more they get hurt. Corinthians 10:10 says the following: "And do not grumble, as some of them did—and were killed by the destroying angel."

The only real thing we get from complaining and moaning is to prove our own imperfection and incapacity, when in fact we are trying to sound superior and more capable. What does a mother gain from constantly complaining and pointing out her child's mistakes? How does the child feel having only his mistakes pointed out? Is there anything to gain in this situation, other than the child realizing the mother is capable and intelligent, and he is exactly the opposite?

What does an employee gain from a boss who humiliates him and often points out just his flaws? In this situation, the boss grumbles and plays the victim because of the employee. The boss blames the employee for the company not growing, instead of taking responsibility for what is happening. How does a student feel if he never gets a compliment from the teacher, who only complains he is tired of explaining and that the student doesn't live up to his expectations?

Another out of hundreds of biblical passages about the danger of proffering contagious words is in Ephesians 4:29: "Do not let any unwholesome talk come out of your mouths, but only what is helpful for building up others according to their needs, that it may give grace to those who hear." See, this passage tells us to only speak words that build up others, according to the listener's needs, not to please the talker's ego.

Certainly, the strongest, most dangerous characteristic of complaining is running away from self-accountability, exempting oneself from events. It is looking at what is going on with yourself and around you as if with no power or influence. It is taking focus away from wrong, unwanted things and putting it in others or in the circumstances. It is feasting on complaints and stepping away from action. It is seating and watching the fire instead of focusing your efforts in putting it out, regardless of who caused it. There aren't too many choices: we either complain and put our strength and power in the problem or act with our attention and interest in the solution. Which seems better? The path that brings positive results or the innocuous path?

Victorious people don't waste time complaining and highlighting a problem. Their precious time is used to solve it, focus on possibilities, not impossibilities and their consequences. When we spend more time with the problems and mistakes, these are the seeds that flourish; the same is true when we pay attention to solutions and possibilities—and often, possibilities flourish so much that problems become irrelevant.

This doesn't mean balanced, self-accountable people don't confront others with the truth. There is nothing stopping them from looking in their child's eyes and, without complaining, saying what is expected of him and that a certain path will not bring happiness if the child continues making mistakes. If a child is not studying, a parent shall not be remiss. In this situation, you need to make the consequences of the problem clear, and not just stimulate and motivate, but demand proper behavior. Not complaining doesn't mean not saying anything when faced with a mistake or poor performance by an employee, as if pretending not to see it. It is essential for the success of the six laws that you confront people with the truth, tell them your expectations and what they actually achieved, speaking more of facts and data than feelings and perceptions.

A lot of people complain in order to draw attention to themselves, even if that means playing the victim and showing self-commiseration. A boss who complains about his team creates a setting that takes responsibility away from him. He becomes a hostage to the staff, when, in fact, he is responsible for recruiting, training, and managing people.

The same way, a father who complains about his son's behavior is starting a process where responsibility is transferred to the child, forgetting that he was the one who didn't educate the kid well enough. A child is the fruit or result of what is received from parents and the environment created by these parents.

Tranquil, fulfilled, achieving people opt to look and pay attention primarily to the strong points, for they know words are fertilized seeds. Like everything in life, the quality of the words you choose to speak is yours: will they be of criticism and demand or will they be compliment and validation? Exercise your free will and speak well, speak prudently. Look circumstances with positivity and clarity and reap the fruits of the good intentions of your actions.

LAW #3: DO NOT PLACE BLAME

Just like criticizing, placing blame on others is a simple and fast way of making yourself unaccountable for the world you live in, and for the events, facts, and results obtained in your life. It is very easy to look at others' mistakes, but much harder to see our own.

Neurologically speaking, this is a great danger, for the right hemisphere, the achieving side of our brain gets the message that the (unsatisfying) result was someone else's fault and creates the following dialogue: "Why change and do things differently if the negative result was somebody else's fault?" This way, a person keeps making the same mistakes without ever learning from them—after all, if others are responsible for the way things are, why should I change? Let them change! Want to see some typical examples of this kind of thinking?

Why change if politicians are corrupt?
- Why change if the problem is my teacher, who is terrible?
- Why change if the problem is my wife, who is critical and complains about everything?
- Why change if the problem is my staff, who is unmotivated and doesn't go after sales?
- Why change if the referee is a thief and my team always loses?

If you don't abolish these justifications and intellectual excuses from your life, nothing will change. I have seen a lot of salesmen coming from a sale—or an attempted sale—complaining, criticizing, and blaming clients for their bad results: they only want impossible discounts, huge deadlines etc.

After all, if clients are to blame, why should these salesmen change? Why should these salesmen use new techniques? Why study, take new trainings, if the problem and the fault for their failures are someone else's? Do not place blame on others. Look for solutions and allies, partners of an eternal learning process.

I met a businessman who, from the first moment, demonstrated his dysfunction in leading his company. All his managers repeated his aggressive, accusatory attitude, which was always to place blame. The team he led was always tense, nervous, and ended up reproducing its leader's behavior. After all, everyone knew that, if they made a mistake, they would be accused, criticized, but, mainly, seen as the guilty party. In the company, everyone did the minimum necessary, for they didn't want to run the risk of making a mistake. If mistakes *occurred*, they found a way to hide them for as long as possible, so that when flaws were discovered, no one was held responsible and punished. When a job wasn't well-done, for instance, the product and the service order just disappeared. The team didn't try to do a good job or learn as much as possible from the job, dedicating efforts only to protect against the blame that would crash all the employees.

LAW #4: DO NOT PLAY THE VICTIM

Lots of people have a terrible habit of playing the victim, be it criticizing and complaining or putting themselves in a situation of inferiority and suffering. But why do so many people play the victim and practice self-commiseration? There are many reasons and explanations; one of them is this: as kids, we need to feel loved and important. However, because of their inability to love or lack of time, parents don't give children emotional food.

One day the kid gets sick and, when the parents realize the illness is a little more serious, they devote themselves completely, with affection, attention, and care: just the love the kid craved from start. Days go by, the kid gets healthier and once again things go back to the way they were: parents don't show that same care, attention or affection, and the child doesn't notice that desired love anymore.

Then, as it happens during early childhood, another episode comes, and once again all eyes turn to the kid: affection, attention, care—needs and desires are met and the child feels the fullness of being loved and important. The repetition of this cycle leaves an unconscious learning: "When I suffer, when I am sick, debilitated, I am loved, cared for, and wanted; when I am well and healthy, nobody cares about me."

We grow up and become "rational" adults, but that child is still inside us, craving attention and affection, wanting to feel important and loved. And to get all of that, we learned the path as children: just suffer or show you're suffering and, allegedly, people will pay more attention, take care of you, and give you more affection. And that does tend to be true, but for a short time.

Like an addiction, these needy, infantilized adults once again will try to sabotage themselves and take their existence to a decline, causing harm just to get the attention they crave. For that, they will show anyone who is listening how much they are suffering, how they are in a crisis, how their life is so hard. They will tell, with amazingly rich detail, about how hard things are at home, the bills that are late, the scarcity and suffering, the abandonment, the failed marriage, and so on.

However, affection and attention garnered this way are fleeting. Soon, other people go back to their daily lives, waiting for the sufferers to do the same. However, the last ones are so involved in that victimization that they are adrift, waiting for the next opportunity for them to present themselves as great victims of circumstances.

How many opportunities are lost because of that behavior? How many relationships are damaged and poorly experienced because of that negativity? If you really want attention, if you really want to be loved, wanted, and admired, live like a winner, act like a winner, speak like a winner. From your mouth, let come only words of life and construction, words that can build up. No one gets attention and affection from other people by talking about their sufferings and anguishes, at least not for a sustained period, unless those other people are also suffering from the same evil: victimization. Then, there will be two emotionally debilitated people serving as a crutch to one another. And that will be an evil vicious, self-destructing cycle.

LAW #5: DO NOT JUSTIFY YOUR MISTAKES

Mistakes are a fundamental stage in the learning process, an integral part of human development. If a mistake is not recognized, there is no learning. And, with no learning, there is no change.

When I read the book of Genesis in the *Bible*, I understood where all the human race's problems started. God, upon seeing Adam lonely in the Garden of Eden, gave him a companion, and from Adam's ribs came Eve. There, they both lived very well, happy with all their autonomy and freedom. God, however, had warned them that right at the center of the Garden of Eden, there was a tree that produced the fruit of good and evil, and that they both could eat any fruit they wished, but that one. If they did so, they would have that knowledge, but could no longer live inside the Garden.

After a while, a clever snake approached Eve and invited her to try the fruit of knowledge of good and evil. She initially said no, but soon fell into temptation and ate the fruit. Eve took the forbidden fruit to Adam, who, disobeying God, ate it as well. Having seen the whole thing, God questioned Adam and Eve, who were hidden, covered in leaves. God asked Adam if he had eaten the forbidden fruit, and he confessed he had, but said it had been the fault of the woman that God himself had placed in Paradise. So, God went to talk to Eve, who, just like Adam, justified her mistake by saying the serpent God himself had put in Paradise was to blame for her disobedience.

So, to sum up: Adam and Eve not only justified their mistakes, but blamed God for their own flaws. The development of that story, the lack of accountability for mistakes and results, is what we see today. A lot of people, already emotionally debilitated and accustomed to being criticized and even humiliated when they make a mistake, were unconsciously programmed to deny and run away from their mistakes, to avoid as much as possible recognizing them, to look at themselves and, consequently, feel once again diminished and invalidated.

It is understandable for those people to feel this way. However, they only hurt themselves by not turning their mistakes into learning, which is only possible when we recognize the mistake exists and are responsible for it. Without that process, there is no way to evolve, to conquer more. To rid us of this terrible habit of always running from the responsibility for our mistakes, it is very important that we learn the following communication premise: "There are no mistakes, just results."

Successful people have that premise deep-rooted in their lives and their attitudes. Accomplished, self-accountable people truly believe that all the bad things that happen to them are not mistakes, let alone failures: these things are just effects, results. This way, they can learn from it and know that, in order not to reap the same fruits, they can just act differently next time.

There is a saying that goes: "Insanity is doing the same thing over and over again, but expect different results." Everyone reaches some kind of result. If I am fat, I don't need to understand that as a frustration or failure; I can understand it as the result of my way of living and eating. And, if I want a different result, I can just change, find another way to see myself, live, eat, and exercise.

If sales this month weren't satisfactory, it doesn't need to be a defeat, for, if you look at it like that, you will be debilitated, unmotivated, and probably do even worse next month. You can face weak results as a learning experience about how not to act towards your sales next month. If you didn't prospect new clients, change and do that; if you didn't use sales techniques, use them; if your body language wasn't that attractive, lift your shoulders, put a beautiful smile on your face. Alas, learn from everything and everyone and, with the results obtained, change yourself in the search for new, better results.

LAW #6: DO NOT JUDGE PEOPLE

When someone offends us, the normal reaction for most people is to get hurt and understand the offense as something personal and direct. When someone cuts other drivers off in traffic, the most common thing is for this person to be called names; it's for people to complain and even make immoral, aggressive, and obscene gestures, understanding that cut off as something deliberate and personal, something the alleged *road hog* did against the other drivers.

This way of living is very heavy and not productive at all. It's like giving strength and power to someone who shouldn't have that impact on our lives. It's letting an unknown person dictate our feelings and emotions.

A self-accountable person does not judge others, only their behaviors. That person's internal dialogue goes something like this: "What a bad driver, that person could have even caused an accident." But a person with low self-accountability levels would say—or else, scream: "Hey, you, irresponsible jerk, are you trying to kill me? You, stupid asshole! Where did you buy that license?" And the person would leave completely angry and annoyed, having their next hours influenced negatively by that other person who did something bad in traffic.

Observe that by simply changing the focus, you alter the way you process the situation. Instead of judging and condemning people around you, you try to understand their attitudes, even if not the best one. The difference in results is impressive.

This way, you can comprehend that people who cut others off in traffic can be wonderful; people who hurt us can become our best allies; people who aren't so true to us can become our protectors. And, if any one of us, instead of looking for others' flaws and mistakes, tried to identify how we can be better, for sure, the world would also be better, with less offenses and more truth.

When we judge people, we never position ourselves in their favor, we don't look in the same direction, we create barriers, instead of bridges; separation, in the place of approximation. The more judgment and evaluation, the more the person who judges believes to be certain of the other's flaw—and the more distant from being their own judge. Analyze the following dialogues:

"John! You do everything wrong! You made another mistake! This can't happen! This is the fourth time I point out your mistakes! How many times have I told you about this?"

What do these phrases cause? What does pointing out John's mistakes and failures add not only to his life, but to the accuser's? What if, instead of judging, you just talked about behaviors and results, helping to bring about a solution and showing you trust in what the person is and what they do? Now, let's see some more productive ways of confronting John's mistake:

- "Hi, John! Those two repairs didn't come out so well. Tell me what you can do to make the tune-up more accurate."
- "This time was a little better, John, congratulations! Next time, let's use the electronic gauge to give it even more accuracy, ok?"
- "Congratulations, John! This time, the service was very good. Our challenge now is to meet the deadlines. Will you take on this challenge with me?"

It's like the *Bible* (Mathew 7:2) says: "For in the same way you judge others, you will be judged, and with the measure you use, it will be measured to you;" or, in another passage, where it says only God can judge the living and the dead. We can only judge behaviors and actions—preferably starting with ours.

HOW TO USE THE SIX LAWS OF SELF-ACCOUNTABILITY

Like everything in our lives, what we say and how we say it is a habit, sometimes productive and uplifting, other times destructive and limiting. By applying self-accountability to our lives, we can opt for what makes us feel good.

With a little rational effort and discipline, you can start to change these habits. For this, I advise you to print the six laws and leave them in the places you frequent the most, wherever is easier to visualize. For instance: stick them on the bathroom mirror, hang them on the rearview mirror of the car, pin them on the office wall or anywhere else that can help you be attentive to the laws.

I have seen not one or two, but hundreds of people change their lives in incredible ways in just one week, just by practicing the six laws of self-accountability. Go, print them, read them, make good use of them, and start your life transformation now. Remember: everything changes after you change.

A person I admire a lot owns a lumberyard and put the six laws in posters spread out through the company, including the bathrooms. The poster starts with the title URGENT! Below that are the six laws of self-accountability. Other clients made them into adhesives. What will you do to disseminate them?

Now, write the name of the person who has been sabotaging your life, your dreams, and your choices.

_____

If you didn't write your own name, that means you are still denying self-accountability. It means you are still looking to the sides and seeing people to blame for your situation, ignoring, whether intentionally or not, the role you play in your own life.

It's time to stop pretending you have nothing to do with all this; that your problems are caused by others; that it's all out of your hands. It's time to own up to your hits and your misses and, thus, learn to do it all differently. Like we have said before, this is the only way to achieve the new results you have been dreaming about for so long.

IF ONLY I HAD THE OPPORTUNITY…

People with low self-accountability blame the lack of opportunities as an immobilizing factor, responsible for the mediocrity of their lives. They say: "If only I had the money…," "If only I had the chance…," "If only my father had been…," "If only I had more education…"

How poorly has the "if" been used… "If only I had that, if only I earned this, if only I were promoted, if only clients were easier, if only my price was more competitive, if only I had more time, if only the day had 30 hours…" The fact is, everything would be different if that person didn't justify so much, didn't complain so much, didn't expect so much from others.

During a seminar for college professors, a Physical Education teacher, visibly sad and hopeless, affirmed categorically that her failures had only occurred due to lack of opportunities. "Unfortunately, luck did not smile upon me," she said, full of self-pity. And the worst part was that it wasn't only a justification for not being successful: she deeply believed that opportunities were left to chance, that some had them and some didn't. In her case, opportunities only appeared for others.

She, however, never asked herself why opportunities arose for others and not for her. She never stopped to think about what specifically these others were doing differently to have those opportunities. Unfortunately, she was not able to realize that others—those with opportunities—acted, thought, and felt radically different than her, and that it was precisely this combination of **behaviors, thought**, and **feelings** that generated the opportunities.

Successful people don't wait for opportunities to arise, much less complain when they don't, because they know they are controlling the boat that represents their lives; they know that everything that happens is created by them, conscious or unconsciously. They are sure nothing happens by chance, our attitude towards life is what brings results, and everything, absolutely everything, is a result of our behaviors, our actions, and our feelings. What we are reaping today is the result of what we planted in the past. Believe me: we are right now planting what we will reap in the future. If I am upright and cheerful, I am certainly planting positive seeds. If I cultivate positive thoughts, feelings, and words, I will reap joy and achievements.

Every action generates some consequence. If I speak, I will reap something; if I am quiet, I will, too. If I am present, I will get results, and if

I am absent, I will, just the same. By managing consistently all your behaviors, thoughts, feelings, and attitudes, positive results will simply happen and opportunities will arise. When they do, a lot of people will say you are a lucky person, and you will then know you have the means to influence your whole existence, including luck and bad luck. In Chapter V, about advanced language, we will see that when we manage our present state (behaviors, thoughts, words, and feelings), we become capable of directing our life to the targeted goal—with a great margin of success. This is personal power at your disposal.

I see that most people who find themselves unfortunate and with no opportunities are in fact "blinded" by their limiting beliefs. These people simply do not realize a whole range of possibilities that bump into them, a lot of times explicitly and out in the open.

People who wait for opportunities know absolutely nothing about driving or guiding their lives, much less about self-accountability. For them, living is merely surviving; they live their lives the way is possible, the way "God wants," always placing blame on others or waiting for others to help or, at least, not to stand in their way. You can be sure of one thing: that's really bad luck…

YOU BUILD OPPORTUNITY, YOU DON'T WAIT FOR IT

Some time ago, I met a veteran salesman who kept waiting for the big lucky strike that would change his life; the idea that would transform his existence. He never thought about it, or else, became responsible for building a winning career—after all, he was waiting for the masterstroke, something out of his control that would happen and transform his life, and then he could give the quantum leap and make all his goals come true.

Observing his financial and personal difficulties, I invited him to one of my sales training. He looked at me with an incredible air of self-sufficiency and said: "Paulinho, these trainings won't help at all, either you're a salesman or not. Look, I have over twenty years of experience in sales and never needed any training."

I asked him straightforwardly: "Then, tell me: why are things always so hard for you? Why are you a salesman in such a small, inexpressive company, with such small commissions?" That's when he showed me he didn't have any self-accountability: "You know how it is...," he said. "If I had had more opportunities, I wouldn't be here. My life was always very hard... Too many brothers, not a lot of money... You know..."

I tried again: "Don't you think this course I am giving you is an opportunity? After all, there will be managers and owners of other companies there, as well as salesmen and sales consultants. And who knows, during this course you might meet someone who can give you that opportunity." He finally agreed, and completed: "And, besides meeting people from the area, I might learn something I don't know yet!" I was very happy about his attitude. I gave him the dates and times of the training, he thanked me with his customary air of self-sufficiency, said goodbye and we agreed to meet at the training.

When the training day came, only chair number 17 was vacant. I looked at the attendance sheet, it was his—that salesman who didn't have opportunities in life. And, like I predicted, the room was full of owners, managers and salesmen from big companies. A world of possibilities, opportunities, and learning slapping him in the face, but he couldn't see them, much less enjoy them. After all, according to that salesman, his success wasn't up to him or his attitudes: it was up to fate to send the much-expected stroke of luck.

Sometime later, I met this salesman again and, inevitably, he came to tell me about the troubles he was facing, how weak sales were, and how difficult and uncompromising clients were. However, he had had an idea that would change his life, a revolutionary idea—and, if given the opportunity to put it into practice, he would be a new man. Obviously, "they" didn't give this salesman opportunity to put his idea into practice and, consequently, nothing changed (for the better) in his life.

How frustrating is the life of people who are not capable of building their own opportunities; how professionally fragile are those who put themselves at the mercy of the world, waiting in line for an opportunity!

These people don't know, or prefer not to know, that these opportunities manifest constantly and systematically in everyone's lives. However, people with developed self-accountability not only realize them but also create them and, mostly, take advantage of them.

Martin Seligman, one of the pioneers of Positive Psychology (PsP), in the book *Learned Optimism*, attests that, the more responsible people feel for the life they have led, the more accomplished and fulfilled they are. Thus, carry self-accountability not only as a life philosophy, but as a strong, deep-rooted belief in your mind, in your words, and in your attitude.

A good way to close this chapter is to make an analogy with a sailboat. In this story, our lives are the boats, we are the helmsmen, and the sea and the wind are the circumstances that surround us, over which we have no control. Be the captain of your life and enjoy the wind, which apparently blows against you, to give impulse to your boat; enjoy the tide and currents that are used to hinder you, to direct you to your goals before the world and the circumstances do it for you. You can't change the sea, the wind or the currents, but you can change the direction of the boat, the position of the sails and the helm to achieve your goals.

CHANGING MY EXISTENCE WITHOUT CHANGING PEOPLE

Some falsely self-accountable people think they should—or have to—change those around them for their life to be as productive and prosperous as they expect it. However, he who is truly self-accountable can stand alone with his attitude and good use of the God-given free will.

Really prosperous people know by experience that it is not productive or fruitful to try and change people around you. They know it would be arrogant and overbearing to go out acting like a wise man, wanting people to be different, propelling, coercing, persuading, or even imposing on them behaviors or attitudes they (the wise man) understand as right. Self-accountable people know that, in the mid- and long-term, the results of trying to change people, make them meet your expectations and act the way you want them to are usually disastrous.

Before we try to change anyone, we should try to change ourselves, for if we can't do that, how can we expect other people to change? I have seen a lot of parents who give their children harsh punishments for getting bad grades as students, when those grades are actually a direct reflection of their uncommitted attitude towards their kids. By the way, if parents were evaluated in similar tests, they would certainly fail them, and with much worse results than their children.

Self-accountable parents change themselves before they try to change their children. They might talk more, be more present, more loving, and even firmer, instead of permissive. These parents could even stop being so critical, so dictatorial, so aggressive, always having the monopoly on truth, things which invalidate their children and make them believe they are incapable and inadequate for life—inadequate even to get good grades.

Have you—sales manager, executive, or businessman—ever thought about changing yourself first rather than trying to change your staff? Have you thought about it? Maybe, instead of demanding your staff to take courses, you could (and should) take some yourself. Instead of wanting your salesmen to be the best, you should first be the best manager or leader. Before wanting them to be objective and result-driven, you should implement sales management tools that give focus and direction not to them, but to you, the one responsible for the results.

How many people would like to change the minds and characters of politicians who are not only corrupt but, often, incompetent managers... However, due to emotional incompetence, these people don't look at themselves and, thus, don't realize politicians are nothing unlike them or most of the population. Domestic personal finances tend to be completely unorganized and mismanaged, even dishonest. People usually benefit from and take ownership of what is no longer theirs, whether accepting extra change or finding a wallet with money, keeping the valuables and then feeling like a good Samaritan for returning the documents.

So, be different: before you want or demand people to change, change yourself, change your way of thinking and feeling, and everything around you will change as if by magic. Everything around you will conform coherently to this new person: *you*!

CONFRONTING YOURSELF AND OTHERS WITH THE TRUTH

Jesus Christ is my great inspiration. He's the greatest of all leaders, the greatest of all entrepreneurs, the master of masters: He holds Real Power and wants to teach us. In fact, He was completely self-accountable. He didn't criticize, didn't complain, didn't place blame, didn't play the victim and didn't judge people at all; however, He did confront people and situations with the truth.

He was completely honest and didn't run away or kept quiet when he found himself before what needed to be said. He didn't shy away from expelling the merchants from the temple. He didn't keep quiet when he encountered hypocrites, running from the soaring wrath, and he wasn't remiss when his disciples went to sleep instead of praying and watching.

This also serves us, who, when searching for self-accountability, must rejoice with the truth, though it may hurt someone, or even ourselves. A self-accountable person knows the importance of truth when complimenting a good behavior or result, as well as when confronting someone's inadequate behavior or attitude. We must, however, stay attentive—after all, we are nowhere close to Jesus Christ in wisdom and sanctity. So, be very careful and discerning when confronting someone. Before you do that, you must be a master in confronting yourself with the truth.

To advance towards your goals, I ask that you write a term of commitment in the lines below. In it, you commit to being self-accountable and using the six laws of self-accountability in your daily life. After writing, you must memorize your statements and verbalize them out loud for thirty consecutive days after waking up.

TERM OF COMMITMENT

I, _____
_____ , declare for all intents and purposes connected to my success and my happiness, that I am committed to being self-accountable in every area of my life. For that matter, I will faithfully use the six laws of self-accountability, which are:

1) _____
2) _____
3) _____
4) _____
5) _____
6) _____

This way, I will reap the following results and changes in my life:

_____
_____
_____
_____
_____
_____

_____   _____
Date   Signature

Congratulations, you have completed one more step towards you changes and achievements. By practicing this declaration for thirty days, you will certainly have deepened the concept of self-accountability and turned into a belief.

CHAPTER IV
FOCUS

People think focus means "saying yes to the one thing you've got to concentrate on". But that's not what it means at all. It means saying no to the hundreds of other good ideas that exist out there. You have to pick carefully.
(Steve Jobs)

When I was a child, my father came home from work with a magnifying glass. He taught me I could see very tiny things with it. And, indeed, it was an amazing scientific novelty for a nine-year-old. I started seeing details in insects, the texture of paper, things I normally didn't see. It was very fun, but the best part of my childish scientific discoveries was when I learned to make powerful rays with my magnifying glass. I realized that under the sun, the magnifying glass made all the sun rays converge to a single point, producing lots and lots of heat. I became almost a super-hero with supernatural powers; with no match or lighter, I started to burn leaves, papers, and ended up testing my action figures' strength in terrible battles with aliens and their "heat rays". What made me the happiest, though, was setting the bread wrapper on fire. The magic of producing heat and fire out of nowhere fascinated me. And, bringing it to my adult reality, I realize that is what focus means: the ability to take advantage of natural conditions available to anyone and produce power, by concentrating your attention on a single point.

> *Focus is the ability to take advantage of natural conditions available to anyone to produce power and generate change, by concentrating on a single point.*
> (Paulo Vieira)

We now realize focus is about taking advantage of the available energy and concentrating it on a single point, producing enough energy to create change. So, it's not that there wasn't energy before, it was simply disperse. Not that there wasn't sunlight, it just wasn't concentrated on a single spot. Sunlight itself doesn't generate enough heat to produce fire on a sheet of paper. However, when I placed the magnifying glass and adjusted the focus in a way that the sun rays converged to a single spot... bam... it happened, fire arose. So, focus is the human ability to concentrate energies on a single spot with enough force to produce change and rapid accomplishments.

WHERE TO PLACE MY FOCUS

The first question is where—or on what—to place your focus. A lot of people place it on making more money. So, I ask: right now, doesn't your family need attention, more than money? Other people are completely focused on their sport and their hobby, dedicating three to four hours a week to it. Again, I ask: doesn't your career need more attention and presence than your athletic performance? Other people are committed to parties and nightclubs from Monday to Sunday. And isn't your academic or professional life needing more attention than festive pleasure?

As you know, CIS® believes in an abundant life in every field. I don't believe that by enhancing in only one area (or in a few areas) in life someone will become truly prosperous or happy. We believe we can (and should) first balance our lives in all their nuances and then enhance them. We believe in the essence of abundance, that to be happy in one area, we don't have to be unhappy in another. If you believe in the saying "Lucky in the game, unlucky in love," it's time to start questioning some of your "truths."

To answer where we should place our focus and energy, we first need to base our changes in two essential questions: the first is about our problems and the limitations to solve or eliminate and the second is about our dreams and the goals we want to achieve. To help you, I ask that you stop reading for a second and think about the problems you have been facing today which are hindering your life and making you suffer. And since the CIS® challenge is about more than just solving problems— it is about enhancing your quality of life, — I also ask that you think about your most daring dreams. Childhood and youth goals you might have given up, perhaps. After thinking deeply about what to change, and so that we don't leave changes wandering in a theoretical limbo, I ask that you write below the two greatest limitations you want to solve or eliminate in your life, as well as the two main goals or dreams you want to come true. It doesn't matter if your problems or goals seem impossible to accomplish. Just write them below.

State the two biggest problems to solve in your life.
1. _____
2. _____

State the two most important dreams or goals you wish to achieve.
1. _____
2. _____

WHAT DISTRACTS YOU FROM YOUR FOCUS

We all have 24 hours in a day, 7 days in a week, the same number of days in a month, and, democratically, we all have the same 12 months in a year. So why is it that people with the same intellectual and cognitive levels and, the same potential, produce such different results? The answer is: truly accomplished people don't get distracted. That's right. And because they're not distracted, they can maintain quality and keep focus on what is truly important, and thus, act and produce up to ten times more and with more quality than their counterparts or competitors.

Considering you have identified important things to change in your life, and know your success is directly related to the ability to keep focus on what is important, I have another PQW: have you been able to keep focus on what is truly important in your life? Honestly, what distracts you from your focus? What takes your focus away? What makes you start a journey towards your target and suddenly see yourself stuck or change direction? What makes you get determined to lose 20 pounds and, after shedding the first 100 grams, forget everything and go back to your former weight? What makes you get determined to exercise and, in the second month, find out you threw money away by paying the gym for six months? How frustrating it is to be determined to be a better mother and, in the first disobedience or misbehavior, see all the impatience and rudeness come back, even worse. How hurtful it is to realize you have been going to multiple colleges for eight years and have yet to finish one.

In *Focus: The Hidden Driver of Excellence*, Daniel Goleman shows that the ability to focus, qualify focus, and keep focus is directly connected to emotional intelligence. However, the ability to keep the same focus until change happens is intimately connected to emotional maturity. What I mean is that immature people can't keep focus on their goals; they start and soon lose perspective of what is truly important to do or conquer. These people are like children who want something a lot but do little or nothing to achieve their dreams or solve their problems. And, with the lack of responsibility which is typical of a child, they wait for someone—or divine providence—to do something for them.

Have you ever watched a five-year-old boy doing homework? Everything takes his attention away from the task. If someone says something, the child stops what he's doing to listen. If he hears a noise at the window, he goes to see what is happening. If the doorbell rings, he goes to see who it is. Not to mention the times he gets distracted by his own childish thoughts and daydreams. The result is that a homework that could be done in thirty minutes takes over two hours and usually turns out incomplete and sloppy. Do you know anyone like that? People who don't finish what they have started take a lot longer to do things and, when they finally finish something, it doesn't have the right quality? Not being able to focus on what is truly important, these people live a life with few, insignificant accomplishments.

In his book Focus: The Hidden Driver of Excellence, *Daniel Goleman shows that the abilities to focus, qualify focus, and keep focus are directly connected to emotional intelligence.*

The first step to become a focused person is to identify this silent enemy called the "distracting factor", which makes you look in the opposite directions of your goals. So, with that in mind, I ask that you answer the following PQW: what are your distracting factors? What makes you stop acting towards your goal? What makes you forget what is important to you?

Below, I list the most common distracting factors listed by students in the CIS® Method training. I ask that you take a pen and attribute them a number from 0 to 10: Being 0 for distracting factors that do not distract you at all and 10 for factors that distract you the most and prevent your goals from being achieved. If you remember any other distracting factor, just write it at the extra space provided.

COMMON DISTRACTING FACTORS

Parties and nightclubs ( )	Friendships that don't add value ( )	Soap operas ( )
Television news ( )	Internet games ( )	Gambling ( )
Alcohol ( )	Unproductive relationships ( )	Facebook ( )
Whatsapp ( )	Other social networks ( )	Pot ( )

Other drugs ( )	Movies and videos ( )	Extramarital affair ( )
Pornography ( )	Only doing what is pleasurable ( )	Talking about other people's lives ( )
Telephone ( )	Sports and hobbies ( )	Dedication to the church ( )
Subservience to partner ( )	Overprotecting the children ( )	Controlling the circumstances ( )
Playing the victim ( )	Insecurity ( )	Laziness ( )
Depression ( )	Resentment ( )	_____( )
_____( )	_____( )	_____( )

If you look closely, these "naive" behaviors are responsible for destroyed relationships, stagnant professional careers, financial dependency, late bills, children who are orphan to living parents, broken companies, accidents, and so many other damages. So, they might not be as fun and harmless as they seem.

I have been talking to people who sleep with their cellphone on and wake up to answer every ring that indicates a massage in a social network. This means they can barely sleep and their day becomes unproductive and exhausting. Other people spend their professional day between coffee breaks and unproductive talks, and don't know why they don't get promoted when other people who have started later in the company become bosses. I also often see people who just watch "a little soap" every night. This means that person spends over one hour a day in front of the TV, or seven hours a week, thirty hours a month and 360 hours a year. In terms of time, this is the same amount of school hours of a graduate course. To make matters worse, most of the time these soap operas tell depressing stories about poor family relationships, such as: a father who steals their son's wife; a brother who kills a sibling and other murders; adultery, kidnappings, violence, children and teenagers precociously exposed to vulgar (almost pornographic) sex, etc. Besides the whole negativity in terms of messages, there is also, as I said, the time loss.

I say one hour a day reading or studying something important for your profession would be enough for you to get promoted at least once a year, and have a salary increase of at least 50% in the same period. It's simple Math. A professional who earns 5,000 a month today can apply this rule about studying one hour a day to improve in their job and sector, and in five years they will be making 40,000. Then, they would be at the top of the hierarchy pyramid, with a highly important job or even as the owner. Do the math: multiply what you earn today by eight and realize the power of focus.

Let's begin. Let's focus. Do you know what the best time to plant a tree is? The answer isn't today, as you might have imagined, but five years ago. However, if you didn't plant one, it's ok. The time is now. In the following exercise, you will identify the most important thing in every pillar of your life. After that, you will evaluate and see if there is any distraction keeping you from living the best in that area.

Look at the example:

Pillar: children and marriage.
What is more important: time and quality time with family.
Distraction: going to a bar with work colleagues every day after hours.
What to do to eliminate the distraction: make an appointment with the colleagues to go to the bar only once a week.

Let's see another example:

Pillar: health.
What is more important: walking twice a week and working out twice a week.
Distraction: watching TV until late hours and not waking up to exercise.
What to do to eliminate the distraction: take the TV out of the bedroom.

PILLAR	WHAT IS MORE IMPORTANT	DISTRACTION	WHAT TO DO TO ELIMINATE THE DISTRACTION
Spiritual			
Familial			
Marital			
Child-wise			
Social			
Health-wise			
Work-wise			
Intellectual			
Financial			
Professional			
Emotional			

Congratulations on conquering this phase. Now you know where and on what to focus your attention, your time, and your intelligence. You also know what has been draining your focus from what is truly important. And you have listed actions to eliminate these distractions in each area of your life. Now, all that's left is to put them into practice and make these changes you desire so much!

FOCUS ON AN EXCELLENCE ROUTINE

Routine means to always do the same things. This is neither good nor bad. However, when we add a second word—excellence—, we start talking about acting, doing the right things the best possible way and at the right time. For us, professional coaches, a routine of excellence is the same as a life focused on what is important. It is the same as producing five to ten times more than the average person, but with more tranquility and time to enjoy all the rest. What I propose here is that we use a tool which in CIS® we call Extraordinary Life Calendar. It is a weekly calendar like any other, but when we introduce rules and concepts, it helps you make everything differently—including you.

Like the name itself says, this is an extraordinary calendar. It is not a traditional calendar with our daily to-dos. In it, there are no tasks for the week, but rather an abundant lifestyle. You will opt for a set of behaviors and habits and, if you focus, it will change your results, your relationships and, most of all, yourself. It is like a map that will lead you to truly extraordinary results in a very short time.

The basis of the Extraordinary Life Calendar is to create focus on what is truly important in your life and not let you distance yourself from it with time. This way, you will produce consistent actions that generate an excellence routine and, with it, an abundant lifestyle. We should keep in mind that an abundant life is that which contemplates productive actions and behaviors in every pillar of human life. Unfortunately, what I have seen in over 10,000 hours of coaching sessions are people who dedicate 80% of their focus to one or two areas of life. Having gains and conquests in those areas, they fool themselves into thinking they have a successful life or they are happy. Fact is that they have a broken, limited life, and, at some point, this unbalanced lifestyle will manifest itself negatively, even in the areas that were initially positive. There are multiple examples of that.

A lot of parents only parent during the weekend, condemning their children to a long, cruel wait to play, talk, and hug. And this time with the children will only happen on Saturdays or Sundays, if all goes well. How can you be an extraordinary parent and have abundance in this area if you only dedicate quality time to your children every seven days? How can you create happy, victorious children if you only connect truly and deeply with them once or twice a week? What will the results for parents be if they only connect to their children every five days?

The same thing is true for the couple who only has time to be together in love when Sunday comes. They spend the whole week away, body or soul, with their attention and intention focused on other things.

Once again, we see an important area of life squeezed and relegated to a secondary place: only on weekends.

There are also those who go to church once a week to atone for their sins and keep their promise, but during the week they don't remember God's love, much less that He still exists and cares for them. We have a Sunday Christian, a person who only warms the church's pews once a week, but is disconnected from their faith and spirituality for the other six.

Following this line of thought, we have the weekend athlete, the weekend friend and the weekend child, who only goes to his parents for Sunday dinner and spends the next six days disconnected and away from the family. Looking at this precarious lifestyle, so widespread especially in large urban centers, it becomes clear that a gigantic part of the world population concentrates and squeezes almost all areas of their lives in just one or two days of the week. They try to desperately compensate on Saturday and Sunday everything they haven't lived and enjoyed for the other five days. For these people, Sunday night is a sad, anxious time. After all, they will have to wait until Friday or Saturday to feel happy again. And to compensate for the five or six days of scarcity, they will likely blow off steam, go over the line in an unbridled search for pleasure, to make up for the five days in which important areas weren't contemplated.

HAPPINESS IS EARNED MONDAY THROUGH FRIDAY

To assemble this tool, first you need to be focused on working on at least nine to ten areas of life[1] from Monday to Friday. This means you need to be a parent from Monday to Friday, having quality time to play, talk, and love this child from Monday to Friday. You need to be happy in your marriage from Monday to Friday, loving and being loved. You also need to take care of your health from Monday to Friday. The same goes for all areas, filling your life with productive actions, behaviors, and attitudes from Monday to Friday.

---

[1] The areas of life worked on CIS® are: spiritual, relatives, marriage, children, social, health, service, intellectual, financial, professional, and emotional.

Now, you must be asking yourself: why only from Monday to Friday? Why not from Monday to Sunday? Our experience shows that when you have a routine of excellence from Monday to Friday, contemplating all or almost all areas of life, Saturday and Sunday are a plus: two days with basically nothing scheduled, when you can live in creative idleness, serve in a day-care center or go to the beach with your family. This way, the weekend stops being an obsession and starts being the extra, the cherry on top. After all, you are already happy and have a life of achievements from Monday to Friday. Right then, you start to understand the difference between a joyful life and a happy life.

Let's see an example that illustrates how the Extraordinary Life Calendar works. This is Carlos's planning:

	Monday		Tuesday		Wednesday		Thursday		Friday		Saturday		Sunday
7h	Work out		Run		Work out		Run		Work out		Run		
8h	Drop children off at school		Drop children off at school		Drop children off at school		Drop children off at school		Drop children off at school				
9h	Work		Work		Work		Work		Work		Visit charity institution		
12h	Lunch with friends		Lunch with family		Lunch with wife		Lunch with family		Lunch with wife and friends				
13h	Call family		Call friends		Lunch with wife		Call friends		Call family				
14h	Work		Work		Work		Work		Work				
18h	Help people in need		Help people in need		Help people in need		Help people in need		Help people in need				
19h	Organize finances		Family time		Family time		Family time		Dinner with friends				
21h	Family time		Family time		Family time		Family time		Family time				
23h	Read about work and the Bible		Read about work and the Bible		Read about work and the Bible		Read about work and the Bible		Read about work and the Bible				

As you can see in Carlos's schedule, he runs on Tuesdays, Thursdays, and Saturdays and works out on Mondays, Wednesdays, and Fridays. In fact, he has a great health at 48 years old. He gets an ok in the health area; he is focused on that. You can see Carlos has scheduled lunch with his wife every Wednesday at a restaurant she likes, as well as dinner with her and a couple of friends on Fridays. Not to mention other more intimate, not so planned moments. So, we can see the marriage area is also contemplated from Monday to Friday. Ok. To complement the social, every Monday Carlos has lunch with friends, to catch up. Not to mention he has scheduled two calls to friends with whom he hasn't talked in several days. With these three actions, we can fulfill the social pillar with actions in multiple days. Another pillar contemplated from Monday to Friday. If we look closely, every night before bed, Carlos reads a book about work and then a chapter of the *Bible*, something he does not forgo. Since it is already on autopilot, he doesn't schedule his daily prayers when he wakes up anymore; it is so certain and routine to him as brushing his teeth. It is also a habit to pray at night with his wife and children. Every Monday, right after he gets home, he puts some time aside to check and organize his finances, for he knows the issue is not only making money, but mainly knowing how to spend and invest it. And he takes it very seriously.

Looking at his schedule, we can see the professional side is also scheduled from Monday to Friday, starting at 9 a.m. until 6 p.m. And he likes that his schedule has a time to get in and to get out, for it keeps him from getting carried away by growing professional urgencies, and his career doesn't steal time or attention from other areas.

Considering part of his family lives in other states, he has scheduled to call his relatives every Monday and Friday. And since he has a mandatory lunch at home on Tuesdays and Thursdays, he invites his sister and nephews. As you can see, he always respects his schedule. And he doesn't forget his children, for every day he drops them off at school and takes advantage of usual traffic jams to play and chat. Not to mention Tuesday and Thursday lunches and every night when he gets home, when there is an exclusive, unique time called family time, during which they all chat, play, study or eat together. Believe me, it is a very fun moment for Carlos and his family.

And he doesn't forget to serve, for every week he dedicates one hour to help people who can't pay for his services, and every other Saturday he goes with his family to serve one of the charity institutions he helps financially. Looking closely, Carlos is the man. He can balance his time abundantly in his life and, with his scheduled calendar, keep focus on everything that is truly important for him.

How about you, how is your life routine? Where have you been able to put your focus and attention? Have you been having an extraordinary, truly happy life or are you always trying to compensate your limited life with short-lived joys in the hottest clubs? How about you **wake up** to life, act and act **right**, focusing on what is truly good, fruitful, and valuable to you and your loved ones? At www.febracis.com.br/opoderdaacao, you can download all the tools in this book. So, access it right now, create your Extraordinary Life Calendar and make the best routine of all: the routine of excellence.

A lot of people ask me what to do if they can't meet one scheduled task or another. It is important not to make your Extraordinary Life Calendar into a torture tool for you or anyone around you. Remember, your schedule is a goal to achieve, a lifestyle to build without causing stress or pushing yourself too hard. What I want is for you to have targets, goals, and for the world not to subtly and stealthily drag you away from the abundance reserved for you.

Look into yourself and you will remember resolutions made in New Year's Eve, which you slowly forgot and swept aside. Your calendar will make sure you don't lose focus in dedicating quality time to your children, making time for your partner, taking care of your health systematically, having some time with friends, and so on. Time goes by and when we realize, we are super far away from those closest to us, far away from life, relationships, and, finally, from ourselves. The worst thing is: we don't even realize it! And when some people do, it is too late. Therefore, the calendar is a way to schedule a date with destiny. It is a tool to, in keeping with the metaphor I used before, be the captain of your life's boat and not lose sight of the navigational chart, compass, and sextant.

To build my life, it took a lot of planning, tough decisions, and structural actions. My wife decided to quit a high executive job and we decided to move closer to our work. We also agreed to hire a personal trainer, so we didn't waste time commuting to the gym. To choose where we would live, we also planned where we wanted our kids to study and where our company's headquarter would be. This true engineering can, sometimes, take some time and lots of effort, but the fruits it yields are invaluable.

MULTIPLE FOCUS

With the understanding of what multiple focus is and how it works, you will comprehend not only how success and failure happen, but also how depression and complete happiness are born in human beings. Then, you will be able to use this *internal power* that is so great that is hard to measure.

In my studies and experiences, I compiled three types of focus. The first one is the focus we all know: keeping attention to goals and purposes established beforehand. This is what we call VISIONARY FOCUS: a clear outlook of the future, that allows you to close your eyes and easily see your intended destiny or goal.

However, as time went by, I realized that despite many people knew where they wanted to go and what they wanted to accomplish, they didn't conquer their goals, or it took them years and years to make them come true. I asked myself: why can't these people accomplish their goals if they still know exactly what they want and do not lose perspective of their target? The answer was simple: they didn't have *incandescent strength*. They couldn't produce enough energy to mobilize themselves, let alone to alter the quantum events around them. The ability to produce enough energy through directed behavior, thought, and feelings is what I call BEHAVIORAL FOCUS.

In other words, behavioral focus is the ability to place concentrated rational attention and strong emotional energy in your goal and purpose. In visionary focus we put intention, while in behavioral focus we put intellectual and emotional attention. It is through behavioral focus that we achieve changes and accomplishments.

You must be asking yourself now: how do I create behavioral focus? There are three neurological channels we will use to do that. The first neurological channel linked to behavioral focus is *communication*, in all its levels and styles. Every time I **speak** about my visionary focus, I am displaying behavioral focus and producing accomplishing energy. Every time I **write**, or have some **action** or behavior towards my target, I am producing accomplishing energy. Every time I **relate** to people who share the same targets and goals, and we invest time **talking** about our goals, once again I am producing behavioral focus through communication.

The second neurological channel to produce behavioral focus is *thinking*. To lend this more force, I can cite the Biblical passage that says: "For as he thinks in his heart, so he is" (Proverbs 23:7). To fuel your mind with the necessary load of positive, productive thoughts, you need to **read** as much as possible about the subject; you need to have books, magazines, CDs, DVDs, and whatever else produces what I call focal incandescence, that is, power of accomplishment. You will have produced behavioral focus when you go to sleep thinking about your goal, when you wake up **thinking** about your goal. When you are eating and the central theme in your mind is the goal to accomplish.

The third channel to produce behavioral focus is *feeling*. As we have seen, communicating and thinking, continually and positively, about your visionary focus will produce the necessary feelings to develop behavioral focus. However, the most powerful way to create the right feelings in the right intensity are repeated, intense **mental rehearsals**. This means: picturing yourself acting towards your goal and making your dreams come true.

As I have said and will explore further, the brain can't distinguish what is real from what is imagined. Every mental image, positive or not, that is repeatedly seen and/or has a strong emotional impact becomes a synaptic truth, a mental programming. This means neuronal registrations produced with the mental rehearsal will generate concrete change within you.

The third type of focus is CONSISTENT FOCUS. This focus is determined by an individual's ability to stay focused on their goal and objective (Visionary Focus), as well as continue to communicate, think, and feel that the goal is real (Behavioral Focus). In other words, consistent focus asks that the individual doesn't lose perspective of where he wants to get, and that he stays cognitively and emotionally in contact with the target.

Talking to some people, I realize very clearly a volatility in their purposes and goals. One day, a woman wanted to make her first million. Six months later, I find out she wanted to become a triathlete. And in the turn of the year, she had a new goal: to get married and be a mother. There is no problem with any of the three goals she had set. The issue is that she changed her visionary focus three times in little over a year. At the beginning, she saw herself as a millionaire; then, she saw herself as a triathlete and, in the turn of the year, she saw herself as a wife and mother. How can a human mind produce behavioral change if there is no consistency in the target?

Another example of volatility: a client's brother had set up a mechanical shop with financial help from his father, who had supported the son's long-lasting love of cars. The company wasn't doing well, so he sold it and traded it for a gym. This business, however, didn't succeed either, and in less than a year he had already traded in the gym for a sports car. How about we stay focused on the same goal and in achieving it?

My coaching experience has showed me immature people are volatile about their goals and purposes. They are led by any type of influence. One day they want this, the other they want that. One day they are sure about it, the other they are completely confused. So, here is a PQW for you: for how long do you stay certain and sure of what you have established as a goal and purpose?

There was a young lady who, every time we met, had a marital goal. The first time we spoke, her goal was to separate from her husband. The second time, she wanted to save her marriage. We met at the airport one day and she was once again completely committed to ending her marriage. Twenty days later, at a restaurant, there she was with her husband, in love and planning a new honeymoon. That confusion of purposes keeps her from achieving any goal, be it saving the marriage or ending it.

Having consistent focus is to stay focused on your target without giving it up for any distraction or temptation. However, we already know that only keeping visionary focus is no guarantee of accomplishment. We also need to keep behavioral focus. We need to attend environments where people have the same goal, we need to keep reading magazines and books about the goal in question. We need to hear audios and watch videos about the subject and, lastly, we need to do mental rehearsals to experience the accomplishment of our chosen goal.

To sum up:

1º) Visionary Focus: clearly knowing your goals and purposes, to the point where you can see them intentionally and sharply in your mind.

2º) Behavioral Focus: dedicating time and attention to produce enough energy to generate internal and external changes. And this energy is produced through the use of three neurological channels: communication, thinking, and feeling.

3º) Consistent Focus: the ability to keep in mind visionary and behavioral focus, for time enough to produce consistent, massive changes. There can be distractions, but you are not seduced by them; you keep looking towards your goal, not losing perspective from the vision of the future.

CASE STUDY

I had a coaching client who, in eight months, went from a salary/retainer of 15,000 to 180,000 a month. Everyone knows that at CIS® changes happen fast, but I had never seen anyone multiply their earnings by fifteen in so little time. Likewise, I have never seen anyone as focused and committed to a goal as he was.

When we started the work, he was already an above-average realtor. Right at the beginning of the training, he became the number 1 salesman, among over 500 other realtors. Soon after, he was the owner of a real estate company who had exclusivity in sales of two great real estate projects for high-class consumers.

Let's understand how CIS® helped him use *multiple focus* to accomplish what several people would deem impossible.

1ST STAGE: VISIONARY FOCUS

At the beginning of our coaching process, he defined his goals and deadlines for each. First, he established his results in sales as a realtor, month by month. Then, he established how much he would be making in each of the following months. After that, it was time to establish the goal for the new company he would create after he became the best at selling the two projects. By that time he would have become an expert in that area.

It was all written down, he knew exactly what he wanted and when he wanted it to happen. He just needed to close his eyes to easily see each of his goals coming true. This was possible because he structured his goals to reach them step by step until the final target. Here is how that happened:

1st Goal: to be among the ten best realtors in the company's annual convention.
Vision: being awarded and recognized at the annual convention as one of the top ten.

2nd Goal: to end the year with an income of 50,000 a month.
Vision: showing his wife the 50,000-paycheck, relative to his sales.

3rd Goal: to sell twenty units of the project in which he was an expert.
Vision: at the monthly commercial results meeting, showing the directors his sales graph and an average of twenty lots a month.

4th Goal: to be the absolute first, that is, to sell alone over 50% of the project in question.
Vision: participating in a meeting with the group's president, who wants to meet the person that, singlehandedly, is revolutionizing the project's sales.

5ᵗʰ Goal: to get authorization from the group's president to assemble his team of realtors who are experts in the project.
Vision: signing the contract and becoming the owner of a new real estate company which would share exclusivity in selling the two said projects.

Each of the stages he planned and visualized happened. Some faster, some a little slower. One happened exactly as he pictured, others happened in a similar way, but the fact is, they *happened*.

For all this to come about so quickly, however, a second stage was necessary.

2ᴺᴰ STAGE: BEHAVIORAL FOCUS

In this stage, he produced the necessary energy to change his mentality and internal beliefs, and also created a quantum move in the world around him, giving rise to an unplanned but beneficial array of events, culminating in the achievement of his goals.

To obtain behavioral focus through communication, he followed three steps.

Step 1 – Speaking, writing, and acting in the right direction

- He had weekly meetings with the top realtors in the company and also with the best realtors for the project, in which he had become an expert. They exchanged ideas and shared success cases with one another.
- He visited the greatest possible number of probable clients, using the first visit to create a relationship; only in the second visit did he show the project.
- He constantly strived for a relationship with directors and owners of the best real estate companies to listen and learn from them, but also to talk about his project and the results it had obtained.
- He took every opportunity to present and, if possible, sell his project. I was one of these people who surprisingly bought a unit, even though I lived in another state.

- He also constantly wrote in social media about his success in real estate, sales techniques, and negotiation.

Step 2 – Thinking: reflecting, listening, watching, and reading about the goal until his thoughts were his vision

- He would only go to bed after seeing his workday results on his smartphone.
- When he woke up, he wrote down everything he would do that day to accomplish his plans and his daily goals in sales and visits.
- When he got into the car, he listened to all financial success, sales, negotiation, and mental reprogramming CDs.
- Every day, he read five pages of a biography about someone who was successful in his field of work.
- Every Saturday morning he invited professionals to share these success cases.
- Every week he dedicated one night to watching a training DVD about what he sought to accomplish.
- Systematically, he got high-value information about real estate from specialized blogs.
- In eight months, he read over 30 books on sales, negotiation, and financial prosperity.

Step 3 – Imagining: strong, constant mental rehearsal about achieving your goals

- Before sleeping, he dedicated five to seven minutes every day to mentally rehearsing all his goals, just like he had learned in his coaching sessions and with the CIS® Method.

3ʀᴅ STAGE: CONSISTENT FOCUS

Together, we created a programmed calendar of exercises for him to continue with the two other types of focus. This lasted until all his dreams became a reality.

WHEN DREAMS DON'T COME TRUE

Being immersed in learning is another form of consistent focus. No matter what we call it, this process is a speed learning strategy, a way to learn whatever is needed to achieve a goal in a very short amount of time. In this sense, it is very important that we understand that learning is equal to changing, for every time we learn, we change something in our lives. When our lives stay the same, it is because we learned nothing.

LEARNING = CHANGE

There is a very simple explanation for people who go through an immersion process and don't change their lives in a specific aspect. Either the immersion is flawed and inefficient in its content, or these people have learned nothing from the experience. They may have understood everything that was said, they may even give lectures on the subject. Understanding, however, is not the same as learning and changing.

I have seen people who experience limitations in several areas of their lives. Some of them seek help, take courses, read a book here and there, and improve a little. But when the symptoms of the problem alleviate, they let go of consistent focus and stop their immersion in learning. We know how the rest of the story goes: shortly, their conquests recede and life goes back to what it used to be. There was no effective change because there was no true learning. This saying is true even for me: it isn't enough for me to write this book to have extraordinary results; I need to put into practice and live every stage of what I explain here.

How deplorable it is to see so many people who don't follow up with something so simple and with such fast results. How hard can it be to establish a visionary focus towards your goals? How hard can it be to create behavioral focus and keep learning? How hard can it be to stick with the program until concrete results appear?

A lot of people ask me how long they need to keep consistent focus for their goals to happen. There is no predetermined time. However, the more intense the behavioral focus, is the less time it will take for results to show.

Another metric is the size of your goal. The bigger, more challenging it is, the stronger the intensity in behavioral and consistent focus will need to be.

FOCAL-TEMPORAL INTELLIGENCE

When we study people and their results, taking as a base the Focal-Temporal structure, we understand very clearly the success achieved by people who started with nothing and the failure of people who apparently had everything. Likewise, we understand the depression of people who live in a super-positive context and the happiness and fullness of people who are surrounded by serious problems and afflictions.

We already know that focus is power and that, depending on where and how we place that power, we can obtain good or bad results. Now, we will learn to move the focus along the timeline and also to qualify it; for that, however, the first step is to understand the relation between focus and timeline.

In a very traditional way, we can see past, present, and future represented in a line:

PAST

As for the past, there is only one way to connect with it: through memories. For practical purposes, we have only two types of memories: good and bad. It is true that our past memories do not represent the truth of what happened, but our representation of it, distorted by time and the meaning we give to the event. However, once stored, the past has great achievement potential in the present and projection potential in the future. Depending on what was registered in our memories, we have a feeling of hope or hopelessness. And these feelings can lead a human being to high thresholds, or even dry their bones. The issue, therefore, is how to use our past to support our goals.

PRESENT

The present, in its turn, is almost infinitely ephemeral, it is a microsecond that never ceases to cruelly become the past. Unlike past memories and future vision, we have only one contact with the present, and this contact is through our actions and behaviors. While past and future happen only in our minds, the present happens mainly on the outside, on the physical, sensory level. There is no way to return to the present, for it will have become past. But we can access the past and the future through our mind and modify our registers of them, thus altering the present.

When we focus on the past and bring memories of pain, we can learn with them. We can learn from bad memories and celebrate the good ones. This way, we create hope in the present and, consequently, bring positive behaviors to ourselves and those around us.

However, if the focus on the past is too intense, and bad in quality, emphasizing negative memories, and if instead of learning from them we play the victims and forget the good memories, the present will be hopeless and faithless. When we focus on the past with right intensity, learning from the adversities and celebrating victories, we live a present full of hope, with the conviction that we are capable. Where is your focus? On past problems and pains, or on victories? How do you watch the past?

Likewise, when we look to the future and intentionally dedicate ourselves to a positive vision, we are filled with faith. After all, we are sure our future will be good. If we are motivated to wake up, work, and act, our actions are productive. In any case, to fully live in the present, it is important to understand how to use the past and the future.

FUTURE

We connect to the future through mental images, a sequence of scenes created in our neural circuits of what we want or don't want to happen. We call this "vision of the future." Even though it is an imaginative projection, the vision of the future present in anyone has immense powers over the individual and the real world.

Unlike memory, which any domestic or wild animal has, the vision of the future is purely a human condition. The vision of what is to come or what can come is the basis of human consciousness. It is our divine portion, what we call faith. If we wonder through Quantum Physics, we comprehend that the reality that surrounds us is, in fact, a creation of the very person watching it with the mind's eye. Therefore, the vision of the future can be positive or negative. Unlike the past, which is a memory, the future is a projection, whether clear or not, and conscious or not, but overall it is the imagination of what can happen.

TABLE OF QUALIFICATION OF FOCAL-TEMPORAL INTELLIGENCE

TIME	TYPE OF CONNECTION	QUALITY OF CONNECTION
Past	Memory	(+) Good (–) Bad
Present	Behavior Action	(+) Productive (–) Unproductive
Future	Vision	(+) Positive (–) Negative

The previous table shows what is quality of focus for the three periods of time. We saw that quality of focus in the past is determined by the type of memory and the meaning assigned to it. They can be good or bad memories. In the present, the quality of focus is determined by productive or unproductive actions. As for the future, quality of focus is determined by positive, optimistic or negative, pessimistic visions.

Next, we will see how the qualification table applies to three types of people: depressive, anxious, and successful.

DEPRESSION MODEL

Depressive people live in the past and tend to surround themselves with negativity. In the image, we see this case applied to the qualification table.

Observing the image, we see the individual's **behavioral focus** is almost completely in the past. We can see that 80% of what this person speaks, thinks, and feels is about the past. So, they search for environments and people that allow them to stay in the past, feeding their memories, which in this case are almost all bad and painful. And we also

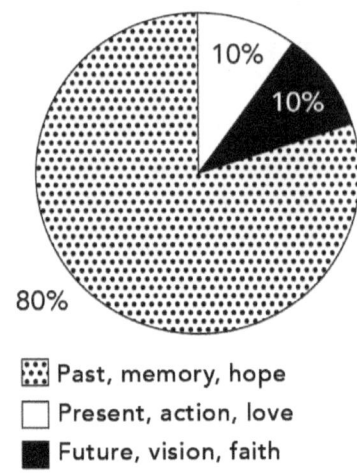

▦ Past, memory, hope
☐ Present, action, love
■ Future, vision, faith

realize in this model that, besides keeping almost all energy in the past, this person is not very dedicated to the present, meaning their actions and behaviors are rendered unproductive. They rescue negative memories and reinforce them with bad meaning. By the Focal-Temporal standard, this person produces feelings of hopelessness. After all, it is hard to have good perspectives of the future when facing and feeding past pains so intensely. In the present, we can see our character acts very little. They avoid doing, coming or going, but it doesn't stop there: not only do they dedicate only 10% of their energy on actions, but these actions, as shown in the image, also are almost entirely unproductive for them, for those around them, and for the world. This way, the final feeling is misery. Present life loses its meaning and the future becomes a scary, unwanted place.

As the Focal-Temporal Intelligence table shows, almost every behavior, action, and speech is unproductive here. Since those who act have power, our character is in fact vegetating in their micro world and, inconsequently, letting their potentially productive and transforming present vanish completely.

Further on, we get to how this person connects with the future. And we see very clearly that they dedicate very little positive time to it. They practically don't connect to the future at all and, if they do, it is with a negative view, mentally searching for what can go wrong, not what can go right.

Their way of connecting to the past has generated feelings of hopelessness. Not acting productively in the present has generated feelings of misery. Facing the future with such pessimism has produced the absence of faith. So, the Focal-Temporal structure has generated internal results of depression and external results that confirm this attitude.

It is essential to be willing to understand that the results we reap throughout our lives are not coincidental or cosmic accidents. There are combinations of physical, emotional, and spiritual patterns, and there certainly is a pertinent result to each of these pattern combinations. In this traditional model of Focal-Temporal intelligence of a depressive person that I just presented, we saw they use their physical and psychological energy to produce negative results. If your result is not what you would like, you need to change. It is all about the results. If you want to change the result, change the patterns.

I once got an e-mail by someone asking me for advice, let's call him Abreu. The e-mail said: "Dear Paulo Vieira, how can I give my best in a world with so much violence and social inequality? How can I be positive in the face of so much corruption and injustice, and still advance and be successful among the chaos?"

Like any professional coach worthy of the name, I didn't have a definitive answer, but I proposed a reflection: "Dear Abreu, I ask that you read the following story and tell me under which command you would like to serve.

Two generals are in a battlefield full of challenges and gigantic problems. The first looks at the past and learns from mistakes and losses, as well as celebrates victories and conquests. This same general acts in the present as though there was a super-purpose to be achieved in the future, doing everything, absolutely everything in his power right now. You won't see this general moaning or wasting time with anything unproductive or ineffective. And when he looks to the future, there is only one thing on his mind: victory. He shares this vision of the future with his troops and doesn't let anyone look back (painful past) or down (unproductive future). They all look up and ahead (positive future). The whole troop knows where it is going and why. Even in war, they feel safe with their general.

The second general also had victories in the past, but is stuck in the memories of his defeats. In the present, he questions himself whether all the efforts and risks are worth it, and asks himself: "Will we win? Will we endure? Is it worth it?" His gaze is usually turned back (past of losses) and, at other times, down (unproductive present), not knowing what to do at the time. As for the future, images are blurred: at one point, there is an image of surrender; at another, the image of defeat; next is the image of the battle and the death of many of his soldiers."

I finished the e-mail with the following question: "Which of the two generals would you, your wife, and children like to follow?" Since I knew his story, I continued: "Don't be surprised if your children and even your wife decide to switch sides. The decision of how to face life and its challenges is yours. Oh, I almost forgot: in your case, it is impossible to switch sides, you can only switch attitudes. Good luck and good choices."

ANXIETY MODEL

Now that the structure and the results obtained with the use of Focal-Temporal intelligence are clear, let's study the pattern of a traditionally anxious person. When we look at the representation of this model, we see a different distribution not only in intensity, but also in the quality of focus when compared to the depression model. This person dedicates about 25% of their time and psychological energy to the past, remembering bygone events. And we know that people who spend time dwelling on the past tend to

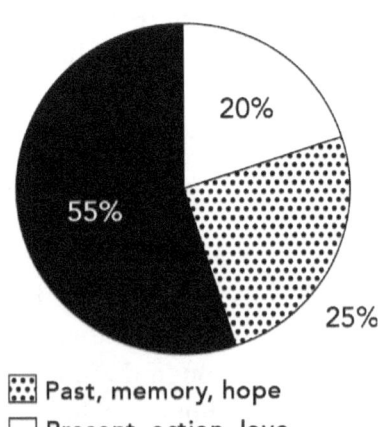

focus on problems and bad memories. And, as we also know, this pattern of memories brings hopelessness in the future and doubts about the present.

Observing the future representation in this model, we can see this person dedicates too much effort and intensity to the future, which is a waste in itself. Focusing on what can go wrong produces insecurity AND since, in this model, the future is an imminent danger, the person with this Focal-Temporal pattern tends to act mainly in a productive way. The problem is that they have wasted too much energy and time remembering the past, and more energy thinking about the possibilities of failure in the future, so there is little energy and time left for successful productive actions in the present.

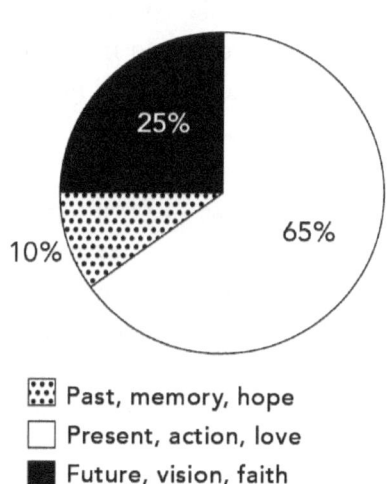

Past, memory, hope
Present, action, love
Future, vision, faith

SUCCESS MODEL

You have seen two traditional, ineffective models of Focal-Temporal intelligence: the depression model and the anxiety model. I am sure these models have sunk in and you are now able to understand the reason for many of your good and bad results.

Now, we will see the ideal model, which all of us want to adopt: the *success model*.

To get to this model, I have interviewed over a thousand people and, invariably, the successful ones followed this Focal-Temporal pattern. My wish here is for you to avoid negative patterns, learn, and replicate the success pattern.

Looking at the model, we realize these people dedicate very little time and intensity to the past: just 10%. And they don't use the bad memories of the past to play the victim. On the contrary, they know their mistakes and flaws, and use each of them to learn and change, so they don't repeat the errors in the future; especially, though, this success model uses good past memories to celebrate life, bringing awareness that victories have happened in the past and will happen again in the future. It takes people to the present, bringing not only learning and changes, but also victories and the conviction that they can do even more.

The people in the success model dedicate approximately 25% of psychological and physical energy to the future. They deliberately create positive images and, in a smaller amount, also negative images of what might happen. They discuss and plan future actions. Extraordinary images of good things are being planted in the brains. The people in this model don't allow the world to determine their mental patterns; they correspond to the first general in that story, they are self-accountable and the captain in their lives' boat. You may be questioning why those people have also created bad images about the future. It is because they know they can make plans, but the accurateness of what will happen depends on the Creator. Therefore, they also elaborate a bad scenario to test what they want and need to change and improve in their positive visions of the future.

Now, all that is left is to analyze the present of these successful people. We can see they live by the saying: those who act have power. They also learn from past mistakes, though, and they plan the future in detail, understanding they are not only acting, but acting right and in the correct speed. In fact, they dedicate approximately 65% of all their physical and psychological energy to action. If we were to attribute one defining word to these people, it would be ACTION.

Feel free to be surprised. Feel free to wish this model into your life and feel even freer to build those results in your life. This model is five to ten times more successful than any other. It is also the model used by people who leave positive marks in this world, people who create value to themselves and the whole humanity.

Now, let's go to the PQWs.

PAST MODEL

What type of memories do you carry from the past: good or bad?
_____

If the memories are bad, what did you learn from them?
_____

If the memories are good and positive, how much have you been celebrating life because of them?
_____

With which of the three past models does your life look like the most: depression, anxiety, or success?
_____

What consequences have you suffered with this model of memories from the past?
_____

Write down the names of three people who live by each model of memories from the past.
Depression past model: _____
Anxiety past model: _____
Success past model: _____

Write down three decisions to radically change your past model and, thus, your life.
_____
_____
_____
_____

FUTURE MODEL

What kind of vision have you been producing (or not producing) about your future: positive or negative?
_____

What is the strongest, clearest vision (positive or negative) that you have in your life today? Does it scare you or stimulate you?
_____

If the visions are negative, what results have you gotten from them?
_____

If the visions are positive, what results have you gotten from them?
_____

Does your vision of the future look more like the depression, anxiety or success model?
_____

What consequences have you suffered with this vision of the future model?
_____

Write down the names of three people who live by each vision of the future model.
Depression past model: _____
Anxiety past model: _____
Success past model: _____

Write down three decisions to radically change your vision of the future and, thus, make your life much better.
_____
_____
_____

PRESENT MODEL

What types of actions have you been having (or not having) in your future? Are they productive or unproductive?
_____
In your family life are you seen and recognized as a productive, achieving person?
_____
In your professional environment, how are you seen? As a person who makes things happen or who is stuck in the past?
_____
If you are in the group of people who act, have your actions generated positive results and is your life flowing? Explain.
_____
What percentage do you dedicate to action?
_____
What consequences have you experienced with this model of the present?
_____
Write down the names of three people who live by each model of present actions.
Depression past model: _____
Anxiety past model: _____
Success past model: _____

Write down three decisions to radically change your way of acting in the present and, thus, make your life much better.
_____
_____
_____
_____
_____

Now, fill the Focal-Temporal map of your lifestyle today and the model to be created in your life from now on.

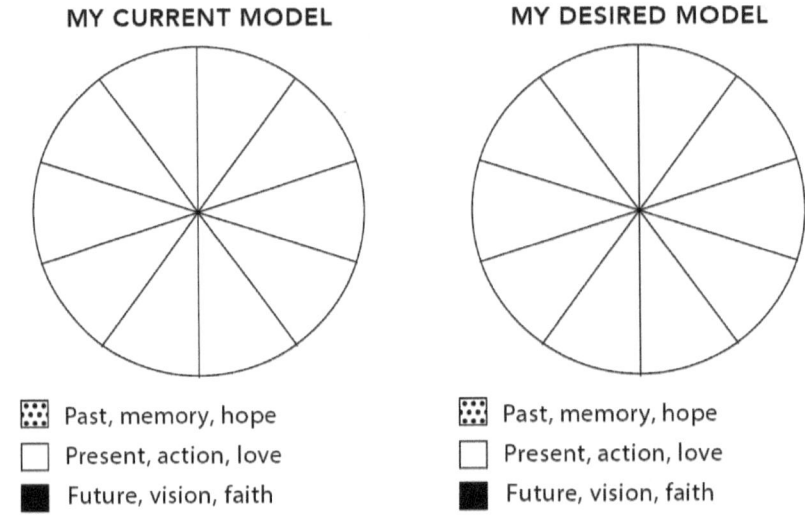

10/90 RULE

This rule is directly connected to the power of focus and states that what happens to people in their day to day lives is only 10% of the whole. For instance: getting into college is only 10%. Winning a raffle is only 10%. Crashing the car is only 10%. Arguing with your wife is only 10%. The other 90% are what we do about the original 10%.

Getting into college is 10%, but the way I will face college and my future career is 90%. What good is it to get into college but never graduate? What good is it to get into college, but be mediocre in it; get into the work market, but never have professional success? So, the key phrase is:

> *It's not what happens to us that matters most, but what we do with what happens to us.*
> (Paulo Vieira)

Being conscious of this phrase has a double benefit. The first comes when we have some kind of achievement. For it is very common that we act like that player who celebrates the victory before the end of the match and, at the very last minute, sees the adversary score two points and his team lose the game. Or like a person who wins the lottery and loses it all in five years, including health and friends. If we understand that what happens is only 10%, we can dedicate all our attention and focus to the other 90%. So, it is not just about being ahead on the score, but being focused on winning the game. It is not just about winning the lottery, but about having the focus to keep what you won and still be happy.

The second benefit to the 10/90 rule is when bad things happen. If we look at setbacks as also corresponding to 10%, like we should do with everything that happened in the past, we can focus and positively expand the other 90% to find gains and benefits. If we can direct and qualify our focus, we can find hidden benefits in big or small losses. It is not the hidden benefit that has to necessarily be more advantageous than the loss, but the wisdom to focus on the other 90% of what happened and take advantage or learn from it, even in pain. I knew a woman who had cancer and almost died. After having conquered the disease and getting cured, she became a much better person than before, in every aspect. After one of my seminaries, she came to thank me, saying it was through my video about the 10/90 rule that she turned things around. And she repeated enthusiastically: "What happens to me is only 10%, but what I do about what happens to me is 90%."

Let's analyze two more cases, so you can also apply this rule to your life.

Case 1

Anyone who drives is liable to a car accident. That is why it is very important to understand that a crash is only 10% of what happens; the other 90% is what you do about it.

This is a real example. Months ago, an unsuspecting tourist crossed the preferential and crashed into my new car, with only 1,000 km on it. Márcio, my driver who was at the wheel, quickly called the insurance, the special police unit responsible for reconciling those involved in traffic accidents, and then me. When I got there, I made sure everyone was fine and was soon asked to get into the police car. I spoke to Márcio, said hello to the distracted tourist, and talked to the judge. After signing the documents, the judge called me closer and confided in me that he had never seen a crashed car owner so calm and peaceful. To this, I answered: "Doctor, what happens to us is only 10%. The other 90% depends on what we will do about what happened." I gently went on to explain my point of view and said that if my focus was on the crash, I would be extremely annoyed and certainly everyone around me would pay a price for my angriness and discontent. If, however, my focus was on the solution and what positive things could come after the crash, it would all be infinitely better.

And I did, in fact, gained things from that crash. The first gain was a great partnership with the judge, who not only became my student but a partner in one of my social works. The second gain was that, with one less car in the house, my wife and I started to ride in the same car a lot more, to the point that we questioned the need for the car that was in the shop. Today, we maintain the habit of sharing the car whenever possible.

It is easy to realize what I gained, the hard thing is to imagine what I would have lost if I had put my focus and energy on the problem. Would I have been harsh on my children, who didn't have anything to do with the accident? Would I have treated the driver badly, even though it wasn't his fault, and lost an excellent employee? Would my performance as a trainer and coach have been the same along that day or the 45 days when we had one less car?

Case 2

Once again, the father came home and was welcomed by a bad grade received by his 13-year-old son. Every other time, he had reacted with a scolding, screams, and accusations. Well, it was until this father watched one of my videos on the internet and, though not believing it, decided to put the 10/90 rule into practice. Before that, the father's focus was on the problem: the bad grades. He would start an argument after every low grade and complain about his son not studying. Then he would bring up all his sacrifice in paying a good school and say that the son didn't try hard enough to pay him back with good grades.

This time, the father had already seen my video when he came across not one bad grade, but a whole report card below average. According to what he told me, when he saw those grades, he started to imagine his worse: this son failing, going to a bad school, not succeeding in life, and so on. Overwhelmed by a mix of anger and disappointment, he started to mentally repeat: "What you focus on, expands; what you focus on, expands." And then came another classic about focus: "What matters isn't what happens to me, but what I do with what happens to me."

After he had convinced himself of that, he looked calmly at his son and said: "Son, I want you to know I am here for you. No matter what happens, I will always love you." Upon seeing the father's not explosive, loving, and honest demeanor, the son asked worriedly: "Dad, are you ok? Is mom ok?" And the father immediately answered: "Yes, we're fine." The son started to look more and more scared, and asked: "Are you splitting up?" "No, son, not at all." Not understanding the father's behavior, the son asked: "And aren't you going to get angry, fight, yell, and forbid me to do things?" "No, son, not this time. I want to say I am part of your grades. And I trust and admire you. I know all your potential and I also know you are more than your grades. And if you fail this year and can't stay with your friends in this school, I want to say you can count on me." He finished by saying: "I love you, son." For the first time, that child showed remorse and hugged his father, crying. It was also the first time he said he was sorry.

The father understood the son's bad grades were only 10%. And that they were also a symptom that something in their relationship was off. He questioned himself: "How can such a smart boy get such bad grades?" Even more deeply, he took focus away from the child and his bad grades and put it on himself. He changed as a parent, becoming more affectionate, creating a channel of dialogue that was long gone. He started taking his son out and spending time with him whenever possible. He also considered his marriage and everything he could change towards his wife. The result of all this didn't take long. After the first test, the son came home looking scared and holding the report card. He got closer to his father, smiled with pride and joy, and then showed an A-. They both hugged and kissed, and I would dare say "they lived happily ever after." Because that is what happens when we put focus on the right place and the right things.

How about you, where are you putting your energy and attention: in what happened to you or on what you are going to do about it?

CHAPTER V
COMMUNICATE

So much pain and deprivation.
My dreams to be conquered.
So close and so far away.
How lonely I felt.
How much effort and how much sweat.
So many days and so many nights climbing walls to get to the fortress.
So high, I fell.
So close and so far away.
How many tortuous trails and paths have I faced.
How far I have walked.
How many fights and how many confrontations.
My giants.
And how many giants challenged me!
How hurt I was.
But on a lucid, clear day, dreams, walls, paths, giants…
It was all under my control, under my voice and under my words.

How many words and how much power.
My destiny sculpted by an artisan, painted by an artist.
A set date.
(Paul Vordestein)

This poem shows the quandary over human searches. Usually, it takes so much effort to achieve dreams and there is so much difficulty in solving problems that lots of people stop midway and give up on the best part of their lives. Here, I invite you to communicate. My invitation, however, is not for you to communicate just anything anyway, but to communicate the perfect language and, with it, reprogram your mind for an abundant life.

More and more scientists show there is great power not only in words that are said, but in the very linguistic structure. As creator of the CIS® Method and the Systemic Integral Coaching, I have seen and heard fantastic stories of quick, deep transformation, and a lot of them occurred after the linguistic structure was changed. Words and their structures are tools, powerful tools, 100% available to anyone who is willing to use them.

What you will learn in this chapter is a complete, profound reprogramming of your beliefs, uniquely through a new way of communicating internally and externally, verbally and non-verbally. And when I say reprogramming beliefs, I mean new neuronal synapses, new mental programs, a new lifestyle, and new human connections. And the result of this new way of communicating is financial abundance, family abundance, physical health, and much more.

Are you ready to fly over walls? Are you ready to peacefully conquer the giants who challenge you? Do you want to trail safe, victorious paths? Are you willing to paint your new life like an artist painting a beautiful masterpiece? If the answer is yes, come with me.

Let's start by defining what language is. Language is the means through which we express our ideas, our feelings, and our wishes to ourselves and to other people. It is through language that we communicate with ourselves and others. However, if language is ineffective, communication can't be effective either. You have probably witnessed people who have trouble expressing what they want. As they improve their language, be it written, spoken, or sign, they can get their message across more effectively. For that, there are very clear rules for each of the 7,000 languages spoken on Earth.

I certainly am not here to teach you grammar, writing, and other fundamentals of language. My aim is to teach you to communicate neurologically on the outside, with other people, as well as to teach you a neurological language with which you can have effective communication with yourself and your mind. If that happens, you will be able to communicate your ideas to the world, to yourself, and also emit the perfect command, which your brain will understand and immediately obey. What I am saying is we can reprogram our mind and change our lives quickly and drastically through our language. Let's now get into the world of communication.

VERBAL COMMUNICATION

I start my seminar by saying that words are like arrows that don't come back once set free. This means you can't take back what you have already said. This expression, which was common in the 1970s, became a mystical truth in the 1980s for self-help authors who, through observation and empiricism, attested the power of words. In the 1990s, neuro-linguistic programming, with John Grinler and Richard Banler, took possession of the concept: "Word structures reality." And since the 2000s, countless scientists have sought to scientifically prove the power of words.

One of them is Dr. Masaru Emoto, from the University of Yokohama. He demonstrated a change in the molecular structure of water through emotions, produced mainly by spoken words. Dr. Emoto proved his point by freezing water and observing it in a dark-field microscope. When good words were emitted, or positive things were communicated to the water, the ice crystals presented themselves firmly and beautifully. However, when negative words were uttered, with accusations and rudeness, the frozen water crystals became misshapen and darkened. What Dr. Emoto shows us is that every word thought, but especially said aloud, carries in it the power to alter reality and even matter. The truth is the spoken word has atomic power, meaning it has power over matter, regardless the intention of what was communicated.

Ancient religions, such as Hinduism, Buddhism, Judaism, and others, are unanimous in ratifying the transcendent power of words. The same idea is also more and more observed in science and academia, in areas such as Quantum Physics, Psychology, Neuropsychiatry, and even modern Medicine. They all agree the emotions derived from our communication are decisive in physical and emotional health, as well as in defining allegedly random events.

With an open mind, let's analyze a religious text, written over 5,000 years ago:

In the beginning God created the heaven and the earth...
And God said, Let there be light: and there was light...
And God said, Let there be a firmament in the midst of the waters, and let it divide the waters from the waters...
And God said, Let the waters under the heaven be gathered together unto one place, and let the dry land appear: and it was so...
And God said, Let the earth bring forth grass, the herb yielding seed, and the fruit tree yielding fruit after his kind, whose seed is in itself, upon the earth: and it was so.
And God said, Let there be lights in the firmament of the heaven to divide the day from the night; and let them be for signs, and for seasons, and for days, and years:
And let them be for lights in the firmament of the heaven to give light upon the earth: and it was so...
And God said, Let the waters bring forth abundantly the moving creature that hath life, and fowl that may fly above the earth in the open firmament of heaven...
And God said, Let the waters bring forth abundantly the moving creature that hath life, and fowl that may fly above the earth in the open firmament of heaven...
And God said, Let us make man in our image, after our likeness: and let them have dominion over the fish of the sea...
And God said, Behold, I have given you every herb bearing seed, which is upon the face of all the earth, and every tree, in which is the fruit of a tree yielding seed; to you it shall be for meat...

The interesting thing about this book of Genesis, chapter I, is that for each thing God created, he first gave a verbal command to bring to existence what did not exist. He used the power of word to create. He did not just think, He did not just wish, as He did not just use the force of intention. He used the power of the word to create. "Let there be light…" and there was. This power to create and drastically alter reality is also in regular people, regardless of age, instruction, and acquisitive power. The power is unalterably inside every human being. The thing is that while some people use the power in words to destroy, others use the words to build. Most, however, use words to stay in a world of mediocrity and impotence in the face of life, its challenges, and possibilities.

Thinking upon cases where I witnessed the power of the word, I cite an acquaintance who almost every day said unpretentiously to his wife: "I know when you graduate you will leave me. I know…" His goal was to hear something beautiful, loving from his wife, like a declaration of love, but the fact is that two months before graduation she left him.

Another case I witnessed was of a man fixated on violence, to the point of binding together every scrap of newspaper with scenes of violence. Such was his focus on violence that he created a blog about it, full of information about each area of the city and crimes that happened in each location. He had the city mapped out and, in many cases, knew even who the area dealer was and his rap sheet. Already retired, he had only one thought and subject of speech: urban violence. You can imagine the result of his obsession and his words: his picture, brutally assassinated in an attempted robbery, ended up on the first page of every news in town. Could it be a coincidence that he attracted violence towards himself? Could it be a coincidence that the wife left the husband in the very semester she graduated?

Likewise, I knew a young businessman who jokingly staged his death with the following plot: he had gone to a faraway location to buy a farmer's car, the farmer cowardly killed him and buried the body in the property, keeping all the money for the car purchase. So far, it was only a distasteful joke. Two days later, he reappeared, and the joke was out. Months later, his cousin and his brother did it again, acting out the same prank, telling the exact same story. After scaring their friends and a few distant relatives who believed them, he comes back saying it was just another joke. Until, one day, he didn't come home. Two days of searches and nothing. Some thought it was another prank, others looked for the young man everywhere. Two months after his disappearance, the police found his body buried in a farm. The farmer was arrested and confessed to having posted about the car sale to attract a buyer and, when the young man came in to buy the car, he killed him, took the money, and buried the body in the property. Once again, I ask: could this whole series of events be a coincidence? Or could it have been created by the young man himself through his allegedly innocent words?

With these two compelling real cases, I don't mean to say these people deserved to be brutally murdered. No one deserves that! I just want to make clear the level of graveness of words. According to Quantum Physics authors, like Fritjof Capra, it is all systemic, all connected; thus, what I think, say, and feel creates a reality around me. We make our reality according to what we communicate to ourselves and others. We can't lose sight of that in any moment of our lives.

In 1983, Brazilian comedy quartet "Os trapalhões" aired a special. The story is set in 2008, 25 years in the future. In the episode, characters Zacarias and Mussum play their own children; the plot is that the comedians would have already died and both their children were paying homage.

As it is known, Mussum and Zacarias have in fact died. However, the coincidences don't stop there. They narrate: "Uncle Didi and uncle Dedé had a tremendous fight and are only now, in 2008, working together again." And that is pretty much what happened. There are many details in the show that, amazingly, came about years later in their lives. To watch this movie and see all the self-fulfilling prophecies, just to go www.febracis.com.br/opoderdaacao. Once again, I ask: was it a coincidence or a creation? Was it chance or did the spoken words materialize?

A lot of people come to me and ask if their words are adequate. My answer is very simple: first, you need to understand that every word is in fact a self-fulfilling prophecy. And I am not the one who evaluates if your words are good or bad: the life you lead is. "What do you mean?", these people usually ask. "Well, your marriage is just like the words you say about it. Your financial life is like the words you say about it. Your home and your work are equal and proportional to what comes out of your mouth." And I add: "Believe me, your life is equal to the average of words spoken by you. So, if you want to know whether your words are adequate and beneficial, look at the life you have been living and that will be your answer."

How about you? What is the quality of the words you speak? Let's use the following PQWs to do a survey of the quality of your words and analyze in which of these categories you fall: people who build and prosper; people who are stuck in a sea of sameness and are impotent in the face of change; or the worst category of all, people who use their words to destruct everything around them, including their own existence.

I ask that you answer the following questions:

Being quite honest, how have you been using your words: to build, destroy, or keep your life the same way?

_____
_____

In what areas of your life have you truly cursed yourself and your life?

_____
_____

In what occasion of your life have you seen the power of word manifest itself powerfully?

_____
_____

Which words or lines need to be eliminated urgently from your life?

_____
_____

A NEW LINGUISTIC PATTERN

PA linguistic pattern is the systematic repetition of the same set of words, phrases, and lines we say audibly and verbally, as well as the lines and thoughts we conjure up as truths about ourselves and the world around us. Obviously, every individual has a unique linguistic pattern that determines their results and quality of life.

To change our linguistic pattern, we initially need to face two challenges. The first one is to cease the flow of negative speech we impose on ourselves. The second is to keep these negative words which have already been said, launched to land, and happened in our lives, bringing into existence what used to be just words. And to cease the flow of negative speech we usually launch upon ourselves, we need to understand that the mouth says what the heart is full of, that is, we talk about our deepest internal convictions and beliefs. So, on one hand, we will change our deepest beliefs and convictions, and, on the other end, we will change the linguistic pattern that not only reinforces existing beliefs, but creates new ones, depending on what and how we speak.

This first challenge implies identifying the curses and, at the same time, avoiding their repetition. The second is to substitute this linguistic pattern by a new, corrected, perfected, and ultra-positive one. The following exercise was conceived to help you achieve a new linguistic pattern.

Step 1: mark the negative linguistic patterns that most resemble what you say or think.

Negative linguistic patterns

- Nothing works for me.
- Everything is hard for me.
- I never finish what I start.
- Life isn't easy.
- I can't take this life anymore.
- I want to vanish, disappear.

- Men are no good, they are all the same.
- Women are complicated and hard to live with.
- Money doesn't grow on trees.
- I'm going to lose my mind.
- What good is living?
- I'm not good enough.
- I'm not going to make it.
- No one wants me or cares about me.
- No one respects me.
- There is no use in trying; in the end I always lose.
- No one loves me, they are just with me out of interest.
- I will never succeed.
- I am not capable of being a good mother.
- I am not capable of supporting a home and my family.
- I am sick and fragile.
- I am depressive.
- I am poor and limited.
- I will never make my dreams come true.
- I won't be able to pay the bills.
- This crisis will break my company.
- Women are unfaithful.
- I will never have my own business.
- My family only gives me trouble.

Step 2: list other negative linguistic patterns you constantly say or think that are not listed above.

- _____
- _____
- _____
- _____
- _____
- _____
- _____

- _____
- _____
- _____

Step 3: choose the 10 most negative and prejudicial patterns you have listed in steps 1 and 2 and rewrite them in the "A" lines below. In the "D" lines, you must write the damages you have suffered from each of these linguistic patterns.

1A _____
1D _____
2A _____
2D _____
3A _____
3D _____
4A _____
4D _____
5A _____
5D _____
6A _____
6D _____
7A _____
7D _____
8A _____
8D _____
9A _____
9D _____
10A _____
10D _____

Step 4: now that you have identified the 10 main negative linguistic patterns and know the damage they cause in your life, let's start the treatment that will not only annul what has been said and the bad results, but also produce new beliefs and mental programs that can change your existence.

Example:
1A I can't make money.
1B Yes, I can make a lot of money. I am prosperous and bountiful.

Notice that line A in the example is the linguistic pattern obtained in step 1 and/or step 2. Line B is the opposite of what was being said. It is a possibility, a new pattern, and the results will also certainly be new. Don't worry if the opposite of line A seems impossible or unreal, just write as per instruction.

1B _____
2B _____
3B _____
4B _____
5B _____
6B _____
7B _____
8B _____
9B _____
10B _____

Step 5: now, we will apply a technique called neuro-association, which tries to make the brain associate negative words to displeasure. It is like giving negative reinforcement to each negative linguistic behavior, until the rational part of the brain stops the emotional part from causing it more discomfort by inadvertently speaking limiting words. The method is quite simple: with a wrist band, repeat verbally your worse five linguistic patterns, and each time you say the pattern, you should stretch the band and let go to feel a sharp, intense, but harmless pain.

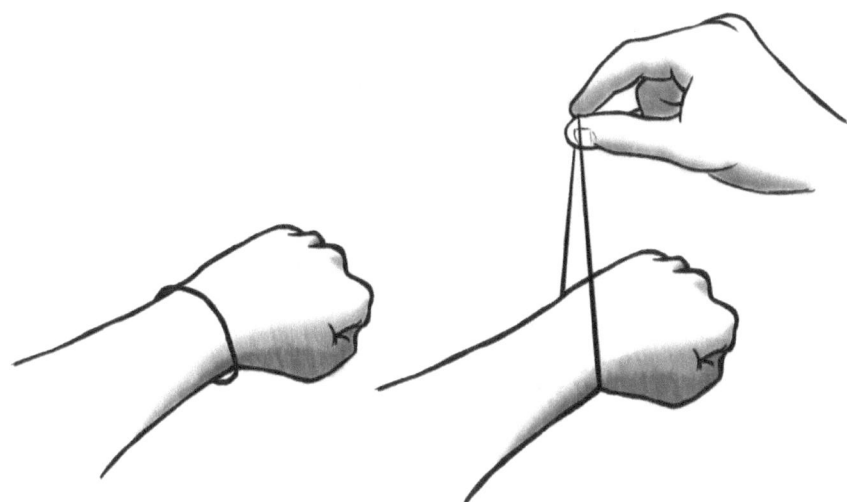

Step 6: in a notebook, write each new and productive linguistic pattern at least 50 times, until your brain, with repetitive stimuli, replaces the old pattern with the new. Then, when you have dedicated yourself and developed the 10 productive patterns, you will have a super-exercise in front of you. You will have 500 lines of belief reprogramming. It is important that each time you write a pattern, you say it out loud at least four times. And don't worry about finishing this exercise in a day or a week; the important thing is to dedicate focus and attention and get to the end.

Step 7: after you have completed step 6, you can still fall in the trap of going back to old habits and repeating old lines mentally and verbally. If that happens, it will be very important to immediately use the wrist band to do the neuro-association after you say it.

Maybe you are stuck in your comfort zone and not willing to dedicate time and mental energy to accomplish steps 5 and 6. If that is your case, stop and think whether you are right now creating tales to avoid doing part of the treatment. Arrogant little tales such as: "I don't need to write it 50 times" or "I'm not an idiot to whip a rubber band in my arm and feel pain." For those who think that, I have just one phrase, which I always repeat in these occasions: "Don't worry. It's alright. Everyone has the life they deserve." If you don't want to do these steps it's ok, but don't think you will experience all the proposed gains and changes. Don't fool yourself into thinking a linguistic behavior of years and years will be substituted just by intellectual consciousness.

You know the price you have paid for the results produced by each of these negative patterns: financial troubles, divorce, depression, professional failure, family estrangement, etc. What more will you have to lose to get down from the big wooden cask and do whatever it takes to change your life?

LINGUISTIC STYLE

You now understand that every word spoken has the power to change everything around you. You also understand what a linguistic pattern is. Now, let's get into another subject: linguistic style, or linguistic behavioral style.

Linguistic style is the linguistic manifestation of a whole set of attitudes and behaviors illustrated by spoken words. It is the way in which someone shows and reinforces who they are, how they think, and in what they believe. Just like linguistic pattern, linguistic style is a verbal representation of an individual's identity. And when we talk about change, we can and should start with linguistic structure, because it invariably has the power to reprogram our mind, whether reinforcing the current identity or bringing a new mental programming or beliefs. We can, in a simpler way, change our beliefs through the repetition of new patterns and linguistic styles. The more repetitive and emotionally intense the new patterns and styles are, the faster and deeper the new beliefs will be.

Everyone has a combination of different linguistic styles. The same way, the results will be different proportionally to their styles. But it doesn't matter what your style or results are, let's now experience two linguistic styles that work as true linguistic vaccines or antidotes: gratitude and perfect language. By adopting and using these two linguistic styles, you will notice immediate results not only in your personal life, but also in your professional and financial lives. Let's go to them.

GRATITUDE

Gratitude is a powerful, transformative linguistic style that has been increasingly used by Social Psychology[1] and Positive Psychology.[2] In Integral Systemic Coaching, we not only research, but also deepen the use and benefits of gratitude manifested in all its shapes. For years, Robert A. Emmons, social psychologist and researcher at the University of California, in Davis, has been studying people who communicate gratitude and the practical effects of it in their lives. According to his research, those who communicate gratitude experience positive emotions like joy, enthusiasm, love, happiness, and optimism, and this protects them from negative feelings such as envy, resentments, greed, and depression. He goes on to state that grateful people can deal more effectively with daily stress, being more resilient to trauma and even recovering faster from physical illnesses.

What this researcher shows us is that the linguistic pattern of gratitude is a veritable emotional antidote capable of changing a person's life in every area. According to the modern science that studies human behavior—Social Psychology—gratitude is an emotion, a mood disposition, a moral virtue, a habit, and a personality trait of feeling grateful, recognizing reasons to be grateful, and, overall, of *communicating* gratitude in deeds, words, and actions.

As researchers Emmons and Michael E. McCullough, authors of *The Psychology of Gratitude*, say gratitude is essential in activating human poten-

---

[1] Social Psychology studies the relationships between members of a social group, seeking to understand how humans behave in social interactions. It studies how people think, influence, and relate to one another.
[2] Positive Psychology is the study and treatment of conditions, such as depression and anxiety, by focusing more on individuals' strength than their weaknesses, emphasizing the search for human happiness, rather than the study of mental illness. The goal is for people to have a life with more quality and meaning.

tial and performance. It is impossible to achieve a high level of happiness without it as a lifestyle. Actually, studies go further, showing quantitative and qualitative experiments, from the simplest to the most complex, always proving the same thing.

In *Thanks! How Practicing Gratitude Can Make You Happier*, Robert A. Emmons narrates an experiment done in conjunction with McCullough, where they examine the impact of practicing gratitude in people's psychological and physical well-being. They assigned three tasks to research participants, who were divided in three groups. People in one group were stimulated to feel gratitude and those in the other were asked to be negative and complain; the third group was neutral. The two first groups were evaluated based on this last one.

For ten weeks, participants wrote a short diary, where they described in a single sentence five facts that happened the week before. The first group should register situations for which they were grateful, while the second group should describe five annoyances; the third group, which was neutral, should only relate five events or circumstances that had affected them—these participants **weren't told to accentuate positive or negative aspects**.

In the end of the experiment, the differences among the three groups were examined in relation to all the well-being results at the beginning of the study. According to the scale used by researchers, participants in the gratitude group were 25% happier than those in the others. Besides being happier, grateful people presented less physical illness symptoms and more disposition to practice exercises. With this result, Emmons proposes that everyone keeps a gratitude journal to catalogue events that inspire the feeling of gratitude. This activity's goal is for people to acquire the habit of being attentive to the good things in everyday life.

Truly grateful people are much more prosperous in every area. The table below shows the comparative results for people with the gratitude linguistic style and those with the opposite style.

GRATITUDE STYLE	NON-GRATITUDE STYLE
Happy	Unhappy
Optimistic	Pessimistic
Giving	Retaining
Docile	Hostile
Noting honors	Accusing
Faithful	Unbeliever
Supportive	Abandoning
Loving	Abusing
Giving	Taking
Hopeful	Unhopeful
Possessing	Doesn't have anything or loses everything

Remember, you are not who you say you are. You are also not who you would like to be. You are not even what other people say you are. In fact, you are your behavior and results.

I see lots of people who say they are extremely grateful. However, most times, when we look closer, we see that is a lie or a self-deception. Just watching these people, we can see both their results and behaviors are far from those of someone truly grateful. I would ask them: do you communicate gratitude as a lifestyle in deeds, words, and actions? If they answer yes, then I would ask them to show me the results of a grateful life. They would have to show faith, optimism, happiness, prosperity, honor, health, enthusiasm, giving, and support. I certainly couldn't see depression, pessimism, hostility, envy, greed, resentment, and it would not be coherent to live in financial limitation, professional failure, social isolation, and so on.

What I want is for you to analyze yourself with truth and clear-sightedness, so as to change your communication style, becoming really grateful in deeds, words, and actions. Looking at your results and linguistic style, how much do you understand the reasons to be grateful and express gratitude as a lifestyle? Answer this question scoring from zero (0) to ten (10) each of the foundations that make up a grateful person.

- Feeling emotionally grateful.   Score: _____
- Realizing you have so many reasons to be grateful.   Score: _____
- Communicating gratitude in deeds, words, and actions. Score: _____

WHAT KEEPS YOU FROM BEING COMPLETELY GRATEFUL

If communicating gratitude is so powerful that it can positively interfere in every aspect of your life—from finances to health and emotions—, what keeps you from becoming completely grateful and obtaining results that used to be unimaginable? Actually, there are certain factors that prevent communication with the perfect language. Next, I will list what usually sabotages our ability to fully perceive, feel, and express gratitude.

1. Feeling of extreme inferiority

People with a strong feeling of inferiority believe the world and everyone around them always owe them something. After all, the world and other people are so much bigger, so much better, more capable, and luckier than they are… As much help as these people get, they still can't realize the effort from others nor the benefits they receive, for they keep seeing themselves as much inferior to everything and everyone. A typical thought by that type of people when they get something is: "This was just your obligation. After all, you have so much and I have so little," and that ends with: "Not enough, you should give more, if you weren't so cheap."

2. Feeling of self-sufficiency and arrogance

People with this characteristic are afraid to say thank you for something they get and show they are fragile and dependent. So, they try their hardest not to need help and, when they get it, they tell some type of tale, in such a way that no one realizes they were helped. Therefore, the typical thought of gratitude by this type of people is: "You did it because you wanted to, I didn't need it."

3. Feeling of narcissism and a distorted self-image

Under this pattern, the trouble with saying thank you is the fact that, if these people accept or recognize they were helped, they will shatter and soil their projected image of beauty and ability—as if suddenly their mask fell off and everyone saw them for whom they really were. Then, they struggle to recognize they were helped or benefited by someone else. The typical thought of gratitude by this type of people is: "I didn't need any help, he did that just to be close to me."

In these cases, people think they are so great that all contributions aren't due to the fact that they need help, but because others allegedly want their presence. They are not really grateful. In fact, they believe to be so wonderful that others should say thank you for having them around in first place.

4. Feeling of sorrow and intense resentment

People with these characteristics put themselves as someone's victim; that is why they are always blaming their alleged attackers for their failures and setbacks. So, when someone who supposedly abused them tries to help, they accept it, but ask for more, saying: "What you are giving me doesn't make up for the bad things you've done."

5. Feeling of envy and comparison

I witnessed a very sad case in which a father—an employee with fixed wage—promised his daughter that, if she got into public college, he would make a great effort to give her a car as a gift. Even though the girl only got into a private college, he went against his wife and gave his daughter a brand-new economy car. When the girl got home, she saw it with a red bow on top and her name across the windshield; she then looked at her father with discontent and said: "Great." She turned her back on her gift and got into the house. The father went after her and asked: "Didn't you like it, baby?" To which she answered: "It's a bright-yellow economy car…" And again, she turned her back on her father. Desperate and in tears, he asked again: "But didn't you like it?" She responded with indifference: "Dad, Miriam has an Audi, Carol got a Corolla, Julia got a BMW. And I got a bright-yellow economy car." The father couldn't hold back the tears and tried to value his gift by saying: "Baby, these girls are rich... This was the best I could do. I couldn't even afford private college and now I'm paying for this car, too..." Coldly, the daughter said "thank you" and went to her room, while the father cried with disappointment for making so much effort for so little recognition. These people's typical line is: "Other people have better stuff than me, so why say thank you?"

6. Difficulty showing emotions

Saying thank you in a genuine, heartfelt way, and not out of politeness, is a way of loving others, as much as a caress, a compliment, or a kiss. Therefore, it is very common for people with emotional difficulties not be able to say it. After all, they can't say I love you either. These people's typical line or thought is: "It's a nonsense to say thank you... There's no need for all that. They know I'm grateful."

After observing and understanding what keeps a lot of people from adopting the linguistic style of gratitude and thus live a much fuller life, I ask that you analyze yourself and grade from 0 to 10 each of the obstacles below that you think, somehow, are keeping you too from being more grateful.

- Feeling of extreme inferiority ( )
- Feeling of self-sufficiency and arrogance ( )
- Feeling of narcissism and distorted self-image ( )
- Feeling of sorrow and resentment ( )
- Feeling of envy and comparison ( )
- Difficulty showing emotions ( )

ATTENTION

A lot of people believe they are grateful because they have a smiling communication style and the habit of always saying thank you to everyone who somehow helps them. But we need to be aware that this linguistic pattern probably happens out of politeness, not gratitude.

> *I cannot tell you anything that, in a few minutes, will tell you how to be rich. But I can tell you how to feel rich, which is far better, let me tell you firsthand, than being rich. Be grateful… it's the only totally reliable get-rich-quick scheme.*
> (Ben Stein)

So, we can advance and deepen our understanding and practice of gratitude. Let's identify five reasons to be grateful for each of the following seven themes. In each reason, start by writing: I am grateful for… Notice how emotional maturity increases every time we can give new meaning to what happens to us—like in the 10/90 rule—and be grateful even for difficulties, for losses, and unpleasantness.

In the following exercise, you will get the opportunity to practice gratitude in extreme moments, when only winners and mature people would be able to be grateful. Write down in the lines below five reasons for each item.

Grateful for what you have.
1. _____
2. _____
3. _____
4. _____
5. _____

Grateful for what you don't have.
1. _____
2. _____
3. _____
4. _____
5. _____

Grateful for what you are and do.

1. _____
2. _____
3. _____
4. _____
5. _____

Grateful for what you are not and what you don't do yet.

1. _____
2. _____
3. _____
4. _____
5. _____

Grateful for simple day-to-day things.

1. _____
2. _____
3. _____
4. _____
5. _____

Grateful for the big accomplishments.

1. _____
2. _____
3. _____
4. _____
5. _____

Grateful for the pains and losses that made you a better person.

1. _____
2. _____
3. _____
4. _____
5. _____

The next step is to continue to communicate and understand the reasons for gratitude in your life.

Write down the names of three people for whom you are grateful and what they did for you.

Name: _____
You are grateful for: _____
Name: _____
You are grateful for: _____
Name: _____
You are grateful for: _____

Write down three things only God could do for you and for which you are grateful.
_____
_____
_____

Write down a ten-line letter to specifically thank someone for what they did and that culminated in something positive in your life.
_____
_____
_____
_____
_____
_____
_____
_____
_____
_____

I invite you to prosper more than ever: to be happier than ever. For that, you just need to communicate gratitude.

Remember, however, that this is not an empty act with no meaning, but an emotional, happy line that's full of meaning about someone who did something for you. Turn this linguistic style in an abundant lifestyle and reap the rewards.

THE PERFECT LANGUAGE

Everything communicates. A tone of voice communicates, eyes communicate, haircuts communicate, gestures communicate, and a posture communicates. Everything communicates, even omission and absence. And every communication emits an external and an internal command, simultaneously. The external command goes to people and the world, taking your communication with you; the internal one goes inside you, reinforcing or changing your beliefs. A lot of people talk about change but keep communicating the same things.

You have learned here to radically change your life by changing your verbal communication. However, we can go even further; we can achieve the perfect language. The most powerful of all linguistic styles. Something that will not only change your luck (literally), but can shield you, your family, your business, and your career. Then, let's learn the perfect language.

I remember the case of a businessman who took his teenage son to a motivational sales talk I was giving at his company, because he believed I could "fix" the problematic kid. At some time during the speech, I asked the 400 people in the auditorium to partner up and look into each other's eyes, say something positive to the other, and then hug. After the first moments of shyness, each duo got into it and accomplished the task. On my left side, right in front of the stage, in the first row, were the business owner and his son. When I looked at them, the father was holding the son's shoulder and saying: "Son, you are my pride, my eldest, and my successor. I love you." At that moment, the son looked at the father and clearly wanted to laugh; he was trying to figure out if the man was being serious, or if that declaration of love was a joke or a well-rehearsed script. Seeing the son take that moment lightly, the father reinforced that declaration of love, saying: "Son, I'm serious. You're my oldest son, the one who loves numbers, like me. The son who is like me in every way. Son, you're my hero. I love you." Then, the father followed my orders and held his son in an embrace.

At that moment, I saw the face and semblance of the 14-year-old change. He got red, made a face that mixed sadness and anger, bluntly stepped away from the father's hug and started to repeat out loud: "Why, dad, why?" Confused, the anguished father questioned: "Why what, son? I don't understand you. I'm saying I love you." And the boy, still at bay, asked his father again: "Why, dad, why?" The father still didn't understand: "What do you mean, son?" Even louder, the son explained: "Why did I have to wait 14 years to hear your compliments and that you love me? Why?" Before the father could answer, the son continued: "Dad, I was in honor roll at school and I was expelled. I got As and I got Fs. I was a champion athlete and I dropped sports for good. I hit and got hit. I did what you wanted and the opposite. And all I wanted was to hear you say: I love you."

In his anguish, the father told the son that, from that moment on, he would say those words. And he repeated them twice more: "Son, I love you. I love you." To which the son, sitting down and melting in tears, said: "Dad, you know nothing and I don't have any more time. It's over for me." Desperately, the father said: "You are only 14 and you have all the time in the world". To what his son retorted, harshly and grudgingly: "You have never loved me; you love your cigars, your wine, your motorcycles, that's what you love." And after saying that, the boy sunk in the chair, crying with his head between his legs while the whole auditorium watched their suffering.

The next day, that businessman came to me with his son, asking me to coach the kid. I said quite straightforwardly that I could coach the boy, but that he, the father, was the real channel of change. Without understanding, he asked me why him, since his son was the one in trouble. So, I had to explain that what the son was going through was due to the father's difficulty in communicating his love in deeds, words, and actions, a dysfunction caused by the absence of the linguistic style of love. The father answered me with a cliché as old as it is stupid: "But he never lacked for anything: food, clothes, school, trips, etc." I didn't hold back and gave him one of my famous lines: "Cars, motorcycles, and horses are cared for by their owner. A son is loved by his father." And I continued: "Taking care of your son is just a lawful obligation. But loving your son is preparing him to be strong, free, and happy in the future, and this is a wise mother and father's merit." I was even clearer: "If you still don't understand what your son meant when he said he didn't have any more time, it was because he is addicted to crack." The father went pale, then red, and, with an expression of astonishment, sat down. "Why, if he never lacked for anything?", he asked. To answer him, I repeated the words the son had told me: "There, the guys tap me on the shoulder and say I'm a badass. There, they say I'm strong. There, I feel important and valued. When I get there, they stop what they're doing to hang out with me. I teach them to play PlayStation and basketball. Everyone there has time for me."

In fact, that father didn't love his son; he took care of him, provided for him, and even pampered him, but didn't communicate love in deeds, words, and actions, didn't participate and didn't demonstrate that young man's value. A human being with no love in the right amount and quality is like a plant with no water and light: their development will never be full. During the coaching process, that father learned new linguistic styles and patterns. He rebuilt his marriage and changed the way he managed his company, but, most of all, used his new communication style to rescue his son from drugs. Today, six years later, the kid is a sophomore at Engineering school and the father's company doubled in size, but the biggest change is his ability to communicate love to the right people in an intense, true way.

What I wanted to demonstrate with this story is that the perfect language is love. Not love that is felt or thought, but love that is communicated in actions and words. Love that is communicated verbally and non-verbally. Communicated love that alters psyche, matter, and the very reality around those who communicate it.

FUNDAMENTALS OF THE PERFECT LANGUAGE

When we talk about the perfect language, we need to give palpable bases for it to become part of our daily lives. Therefore, I present a fundamental characteristic of this language: **content**, and consequently, feelings produced by it. I modeled, mapped, and researched the language of masters in the art of leading and connecting positively and productively with other people, and then didactically united these characteristics, which I will now present.

Content is about what happens to the people with whom we are trying to communicate. It is like the message in an e-mail being read by the receiver. However, it's not just any kind of message or any content that can produce the perfect language. The perfect language is based on four fundamentals: **belonging**, **importance**, **meaning**, and **distinction**. These linguistic fundamentals build or destroy, approximate or drive away, heal or sicken, motivate or unmotivated. And, literally, these contents can kill or save. Every day, cases of exaggerated and violent reactions in the streets proliferate, as people yell and curse at each other after feeling wronged. In situations like that, words can generate physical aggression and even death. How many stories haven't we heard from people who killed themselves after being verbally abused by their spouse or parent? Once again, actions come from words.

Events that happen to us are connected, they are quantum. Sometimes, it is hard to realize these connections, but, in some opportunities they manifest and result in immediate action and reaction: right after we mention an event, for example, it happens. That is why one mustn't forget the power of our words in our lives and the lives of others.

Parents, leaders, spouses, friends, teachers, trainers, and children who effectively play their role, communicate by giving people the conviction of being part of something bigger (of belonging). Something that shelters, supports, and protects them, clearly showing them, they are part of a relationship, they are part of a company, they integrate a group, and so on. These people who master the perfect language show others around them that they are not alone in the world (belonging).

Can you imagine what it means to be a receiver of that communication pattern? These people who are effective in their role also use their verbal speech and body expression to show others how important and relevant they are, how they make a difference (importance).

It doesn't stop there; the masters' content language also makes people around them realize the true meaning of what they do, and even the meaning of life itself. To crown the effectiveness of the perfect language content, these people don't treat others as one of many, quite the opposite: they make their partners feel unique and different (distinction).

When there is meaning in language, I show my part as well as the others' part in the world. I, as a father, show with my language the meaning of my son's life, I show that his life has a purpose, a direction, a reason, so he knows he is not just passing through this world. Next, you will read examples of the perfect language content for different people.

Example 1: children

Picture a child's perception when feeling how important they are in their father's protecting hug. And how it is for a child for their parents' bedroom door to always (or almost always) be open at night, when the boogie man comes to scare them. Imagine what it means for this child, even if they don't stay or sleep in that bedroom, to feel accepted and belonging to that place and to those people; not to feel on the outside looking in, exposed to animals, to bad guys, and to threats; but to be inside, where the important people who give the orders live.

Example 2: employees

Consider the perspective of an employee who sees in his boss's words and attitudes that show he is important, and not only that, but he also belongs to that company. Consider his feelings in knowing they are together helping to build a better world; that all his effort and hard work is not only about money, but a life calling. Everything is clear to this employee: "I am not a hired hand or resource; I am the company itself." And even in the middle of many other employees, his boss can identify him and call him by his name.

Example 3: spouse

When a husband or wife feel the house belongs to them and that they are a strong link in what they call a home, they start to emanate a bigger, different glow. To do their part, it is essential for them to tell by their spouse's words and tone of voice that they are special, different, unique. When the husband or wife show with deeds, actions, and words that their spouse is loved the way they are and that the ring they carry on their finger has a bigger meaning, naturally the other one becomes the soul of the house. And they can confirm the real meaning of life when they hear their children call them by their name: mom or dad.

Example 4: friend

When someone looks at their friends and calls them brothers, and together they share the same speech and interests, it is extraordinary. It is like being in a tribe, being equal but also distinct from the rest. It is like having a special, exclusive passport that only that dynasty can have. It is giving life meaning.

Example 5: teacher/trainer

How bad it is to believe our teacher is an unattainable being who belongs to the world of knowledge, while we belong to the world of ignorance. Some teachers/trainers distance themselves from their students by putting themselves on the highest pedestals, where many young people don't dare to go. When I am ministering my events, I make sure to be close to the students, to get down from the stage, walk among them, touch them. Look them in the eyes and use "we", in the place of "you" and "I". Nothing gives me greater pleasure than being able to hug my students by the end of a fifteen-hour or a three-day training and hear what they have to say. But, overall, nothing should be more important to a teacher than realizing how much he can learn from each and every student. Words can produce learning, enthusiasm, and integration. One of my students once asked me why I didn't give up on him. My answer was very simple: "You matter to me, Febracis is your home, and I am sure that everything you went through means you are part of something bigger. Be sure there is something to learn from all this. Soon ahead you will use all this painful learning to prosper and help many people around you." Crying with emotion, he hugged me and, soon after, there he was, simply living up to these words.

Compare your language to the same category of people in the listed example and answer: What have you been communicating to your parents, the cloth from which you were cut? How have you been treating your staff or coworkers? And your spouse, how does he or she feel about you?

I invite you to fill the table below and score them 0 to 10, according to the way you use your language content to communicate with the main categories of people in your life. See that there are two blank columns where you can insert the people or other categories of people who are important for you.

Tabela conteúdos linguísticos x categorias Humanas

	Spouse	Parents	Children	Close people	Friends	Coworkers		
Belonging								
Importance								
Meaning								
Distinction								
Total								

After you evaluate yourself in each of the four contents, tally your scores and evaluate the total for each human category. The highest score is 40 and the lowest is 0. Looking at the quality of communication, you can understand two things: The first is the quality and results of your own life, the second is the quality of your relationships. Based on this evaluation and the practical results you have been experimenting, all that is left is to ask: How will you achieve perfect language with each of these people or categories of people, to experience the best relationship and the best life? Write below your decisions about each of the table's columns.

1. Spouse: _____
2. Parents: _____
3. Children: _____
4. Close people : _____
5. Friends: _____
6. Coworkers: _____
7. _____ : _____
8. _____ : _____

COMMUNICATION OF LIGHT OR DARK

Besides the quality of the four contents, what do you usually communicate to the people related above? Do you communicate peace, joy, acceptance, love, affection, care, self-love? Or would that be indifference, lack of time, anger, impatience, moodiness, fear, insecurity, family disunion? Honestly, what have you been communicating to those closest to you?

That father and businessman I referred to earlier planted words and actions and reaped all kinds of trouble with his son and in his own life. When he decided to plant different things, he again got results, but the fruits were quite different.

Looking at the following table, observe that on the right side there are five words. I ask that as you read the explanation, you complete the table.

Dark side		**Light side**
_____	_____	_____ God
_____	_____	_____ Certainty
_____	_____	_____ Peace
_____	_____	_____ Love
-10	0	10

The first task is to fill in on the left side, with the opposites of the words on the right side of the table. For example, starting from the bottom up, we have the word *love*; what word is opposite to *love*? How about *hate*? If you agree the opposite of love is *hate*, I ask that you write that on the left side, in the same line. If you feel something else is opposed to the word *love*, feel free to put in what you think is best. Then, if there is *love* on one side and *hate* on the other, what word would go between them? How about *indifference* or *estrangement*? If you agree, I ask that you write that word, or another you feel is more appropriate, in the center of the table, in the same line as love and *hate*.

Going up one line, what word is opposite to *life*? How about *death*? If you agree with the word *death* as the opposite to the word *life*, write that down above *hate*. And in the middle, between *life* and *death*, what word would fit? How about *illness*? If you think it is something else, write that down. Now, let's take *peace*. What word opposite to *peace* would you put on the far left? *Unrest or disquiet*? Write down what you think is best. And in the middle of the two, how about *stress*? In the conviction line, would the opposite word be *doubt*? In the middle, how about *fear*?

Finally, we get to the first line: *God*. If He is on the far right, what is the natural opposite to *God* and you would place on the far left? *Devil*? *Evil Force*? So, write down in the extreme left what you believe to correspond to the opposite of God. And in between, whatever fits? Lack of faith? Fill it according to what you feel to be more appropriate.

Observe that we have created this table together, and think about your love life. Think about yourself, your loved one, and your relationship, and use a pen to make a mark somewhere in between the 10 on the far right and the -10 on the far left, showing how your communication with this person is on each of the five lines. Be honest and score your communication to that person in terms of love. If it involves constancy, love and honesty, your mark will definitely be close to 10. However, if you are sometimes impatient and rude, under stress, or are somewhat distant, your score will probably not go beyond the middle of the table. Do the same evaluation regarding your parents, if you still have them, or for their memory; do it regarding your children. Do you communicate love (right side), distance (middle) or anger and impatience (left side)? Do this evaluation regarding all your connections and ask yourself what you have in fact been communicating to these people who are so important in your life.

I want to take this opportunity to invite you to do another analysis: if God and His complements or synonyms are on the right side, and the devil and his complements or synonyms are on the left, what side have you been playing? Who have you been pleasing with your communication, God or His opposite? This table can become a veritable map of cause and effect, where you can measure your current communication and know what results to expect in your life. Lastly, in which side have you been walking with your communication: The light side or the dark side?

WHEN LOVE DOESN'T WORK

A 50-year-old woman came to me and, in an accusing tone, said life wasn't as simple as I said, and she was proof. Very patiently, I asked her to explain it further, giving me more details so I could understand. Grieving, she told me her life story.

"Paulo, I'm 50 years old and got married at 25. My husband asked me to drop out of college and I did. Since he didn't like my family, I also distanced myself from my relatives. He was very jealous and, to avoid any problems, I also distanced myself from my friends and never had a job. We had three children and for 25 years I was a full-time stay-at-home mother and wife. And now that I'm 50, my husband left me for a 25-year-old. How can you say love conquers all? How can you say love shields our family? How can you say that, if all I did my whole life was love and care for that man? And look where it got me. Now I'm here, old, ugly, and dumped."

As an answer, I used the second commandment in the Bible: "You shall love your neighbor as yourself." After citing that passage, I asked: "Have you loved your husband as much as you loved yourself? Have you committed to your tasks at home in the same proportion that you have committed to yourself? Have you loved yourself at all over these 25 years?

Have you respected and taken care of yourself during that time? Have you presented yourself as worthy, important, or as a worthless woman, a servant with no needs or wills of her own?". I continued: "A plane needs both wings to fly, just like a relationship needs one person to love the other as much as they love themselves to work.

So, don't take this the wrong way," I said with compassion as she started to come to her senses, "but the problem isn't your husband who left you or the 25-year-old who is with him, the problem is you. The problem is that you don't respect yourself, don't value yourself, you see yourself as an inferior being." I kept going, with all the love and firmness that the situation demanded: "How would your life be if you had stayed close to your parents and siblings? How would your life be if you had graduated and built a career? How would your life be if you had set boundaries and said no at the right time? How would your life be if you had communicated self-love?" She cried, hugged me, and said it was all true. I was sorry for her, and advised: "Your day is now and now is the time for you to go back to college, take care of your body, reclaim friendships, and visit places you've never seen. Now is the time to start loving yourself and living."

How about your plane, does it have one wing or two? Do you communicate intense love to others and to yourself or more love to others than to yourself? Or do you love yourself more than others? For your plane to take off and stay high even amidst storms, you need to keep focus: "Love my neighbors as I love myself." For communicating love will always be the best strategy, as long as it is done right.

THE LOSADA RATIO

Most people believe they should only compliment someone when that person has done something useful or well-done. It is the give-and-take logic. These people say: "Why would I compliment someone on just doing their job?" or "Too many compliments spoil everything." Once, I got home with an unprecedented feat: An A in the Math test. All proud and looking for approval, I ran to my father holding the test and, when I showed it to him, he answered dismissively: "That was no more than your duty, after all, you're a professional student." That answer rang deep and hurt me a lot. I had tried very hard to please my parents and it just didn't work.

Now, I know he meant well, believing that if he said that was no more than a duty, I might show a more focused behavior towards my studies and dedicate myself more. However, with the advancement of the human performance science, brain mapping through functional MRI, Positive Psychology, and coaching, we now know that when it comes to human performance, the opposite is true: first, you compliment, then you get a great performance. While a traditional leader waits for their employees to do something well and then compliment them, the high-performing business leader compliments first and, as a consequence, their subordinates perform much better. Unlike an unaware parent, those who know how to get the best performance out of their children use modern metrics: they compliment first and, as a consequence, see a great behavior.

This new metric is part of a scientific research called the Losada Ratio, named after its creator, psychologist Marcial Losada. This Chilean scientist conducted mathematical experiences in which people who performed highly in human relationships compliment or connect to others following a proportion of positive and negative interactions. According to Losada, complimenting or positively connecting to others is not enough to get the best out of a relationship; you need to follow a mathematical model. After numerous simulations, he found a ratio of positive and negative interactions to keep any relationship at a minimal level of quality. The minimum proportion is three positive interactions to one negative. These positive interactions can be any type of verbal or non-verbal communication, a formal compliment, a pat on the back, a smile, even positive gestures or letters. The important thing is for that positive communication to be recognized by those who received it as in fact positive. Negative interaction can be a verbal reprimand, a harsh feedback, a critical gesture, a disappointed look, and even a demonstration of indifference.

If the three to one ratio, meaning three positive communications/interactions for each negative one, keeps the relationship and results at a minimal quality, the Losada mathematical model shows that, when you increase positive interactions to four and keep one negative, the person that receives the interactions has an even better performance. Observing the following graph, we can follow the ratio of positive versus negative communication and the change in human performance. As the ratio of positive interaction increases, the result follows positively. And the best performance is from six to eight positive interactions to each negative one. However, if the ratio of positive interactions increases beyond that, performance starts to decrease. We can see that if positive interactions go further than eleven positives to one negative, performance again goes beyond the minimum acceptable level.

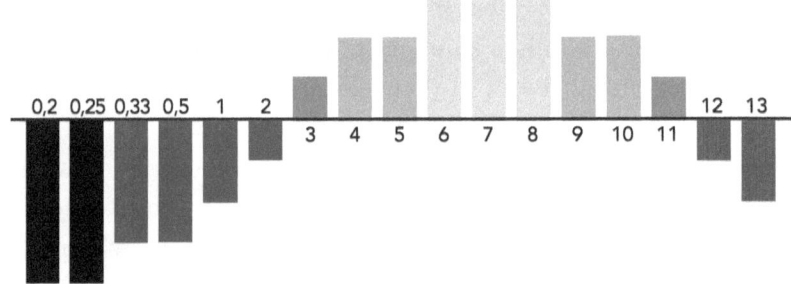

Based on Losada's mathematical model, it is very easy to evaluate results in any type of relationship. You can just mark on a sheet of paper the ratio of positive to negative interactions between people for a while. I watched this couple closely and could see the change in interactions early enough to predict the events and the relationship's closure. At the beginning, they had over ten positive interactions to each negative one. Over time, the ratio changed and fell to seven positives and one negative. Back then, people around them said the relationship was more mature. With more time, the proportion decreased to five positives to one negative. Later, I observed it had fallen to three positives to one negative. At that moment, the marriage was apparently normal, and few people could realize the troubles between them. In our next meeting, I counted two positive interactions to one negative; it was clear to me that their relationship was coming to an end. Soon after, my wife brought the news that their marriage had ended.

You can evaluate the performance and relationship between parents and children the same way. When parents compliment too much, above ten or eleven positive interactions to one negative, we see spoiled, willful children, stuck in a comfort zone created by their own parents. When we see children fustigated with an avalanche of negative communication, such as criticism, reproaches, or indifference, again we see low performance, learning deficit, attention deficit, or hyperactivity. These children are generally motivated to doing just the bare minimum, in order not to be criticized or reproached anymore.

We know the power of words, we know they can mean life and death, they can build and destroy, bring love and misery, forgive and accuse. Remember the first chapter in the book of Genesis, mentioned in this chapter. For the universe to exist, God didn't just think or imagine it: He spoke, He gave a verbal command, and only then did life start.

Now, we can use the power of words within this ratio to project and produce growth in any human interaction. How about using the Losada Ratio to restore your marriage? How about using this ratio to rescue your children from delinquency, drugs, precocious sex, or just family estrangement? What if you could increase your professional staff's results just by putting the Losada metric into practice?

POWERFUL WISDOM QUESTIONS

Who have you been failing the most in using the Losada Ratio, with a proportion inferior to three positive interactions to one negative?

_____
_____

List three people to start applying the Losada Ratio and change your relationship and results. Who are they?

_____
_____
_____

With what social group have you gotten the Losada Ratio right more often?

_____
_____
_____

NON-VERBAL COMMUNICATION

Every communication is made up of verbal and non-verbal ingredients. In practice, it is impossible to separate one from the other. It would be like separating flour from sugar in a cake that is ready. However, for better understanding, let's treat both forms of communication separately.

While verbal communication can be summed up by spoken words, non-verbal includes all gestures, postures, vocal tone, facial expressions, and so on. And our saying is still valid: we can change our lives and our results by changing our verbal and non-verbal communication.

Just like there is a verbal linguistic pattern, there is also a non-verbal linguistic pattern. As you already know, everyone has their own unique linguistic pattern that tells the world who they are and reinforces their identity beliefs—and the results people experience in their lives are directly derived from that. Good patterns generate good results; bad patterns generate bad results. Some people have non-verbal patterns of sadness, other people have non-verbal patterns of success, others yet have non-verbal patterns of stress and problems. Some have non-verbal patterns of victimization and impotence. What is your non-verbal linguistic pattern? What non-verbal information or commands do you systematically send your brain saying who you are, what you are capable of or how much you deserve good things?

When I see people with negative results in some area of their lives, I know they have a deficient linguistic pattern in that specific area. All it would take is redoing or changing the linguistic pattern for results to immediately change. So, we can look at our lives and results and understand we didn't fail, just obtained bad results. When someone isn't accepted for a job, this isn't a failure, but a bad result. When a player misses a penalty, this also isn't a failure, but a bad result. I like to believe there are no failures. And since everything in this case is a bad result, let's learn how to use communication to change our bad results and, especially, who we are.

> *We know our minds change our bodies, what we didn't know is our bodies change our minds even faster. And power-posing for a few minutes can really change your life significantly, increasing your testosterone and lowering your cholesterol.*
> (Amy Cuddy)

Another scientific experiment by researcher Robert A. Emmons drastically changed what was believed about non-verbal communication and human performance. The experiment took three groups of people, who got the same text to read and evaluate if it was optimistic or pessimistic. However, the first group should read it with a pen in their mouth, as if they were pouting. The second group should read it without the pen in their mouth. The third group should also read it with then pen in their mouth, but stuck between their molars, simulating a smile. Look at the following drawing.

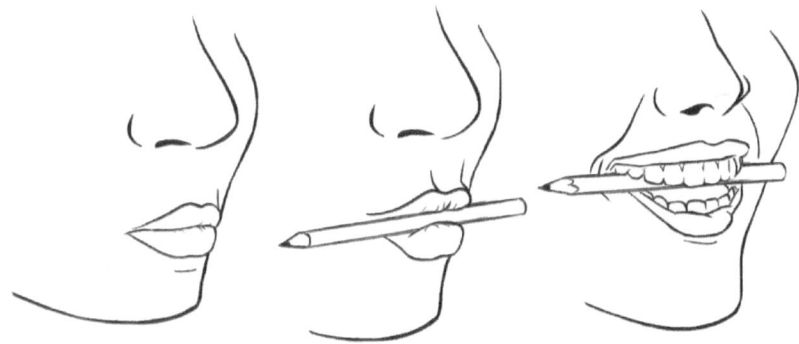

After several rounds of the experiment, in all of them, it was proven that the group that held the pen with lips simulating a pout interpreted the text with the most pessimistic score of all three. The group who read it with the pen between their molars, simulating a smile, gave the text the most optimistic score. And the control group who read the text with no pen gave the text an intermediate score. The experiment decisively showed that a small, subtle change in non-verbal communication alters how a person sees and notices the world around them. In this study, a small change in the lips was enough for a different input. And, if the input changes, the output will certainly change, too.

It is tremendous to realize that just a change in facial expression was responsible for a new way of seeing the world. Thus, if we can make our subtle non-verbal communication positive for enough time, what will happen to us and our results? The idea is that we can change our results immediately simply by altering small nuances in our non-verbal communication. How about starting now? Try doing the same experience of the pen in the mouth yourself and you will see what happens to your state of mind right away.

The following drawing shows five different postures in the same person, from completely bent to completely erect and lofty.

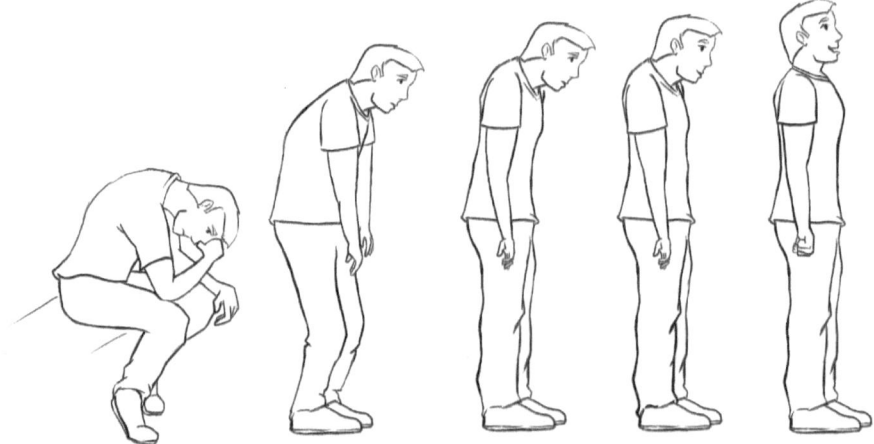

Neuroscience shows that, even though it is the same person in different postures, performance and results will vary from one posture to the other. Looking at the first drawing, we can see an emotionally limited man who lives well below his best potential; he's wrapped in problems, and probably playing the victim. However, as he gets more erect, elevates his shoulders, and lifts his head, his brain immediately responds with new emotional molecules. Then he gets to his highest potential with a completely erect posture. You already know, but I will state this again: With each posture, the person produces different results. So, results aren't coincidences, but consequences. Which of these postures your average body communication displays the most? How about carrying out a survey with people of your social and professional circles and asking them to signal which posture resembles yours?

Do this experiment: go to a silent, private place and adopt one of the five postures for two minutes without losing focus and concentration, take into account that facial communication and body language must be coherent. Then, write in the following lines all the results you notice in your thoughts and feelings when communicating each of them.

Posture 1

Posture 2

Posture 3

Posture 4

Posture 5

Once, in one of my events, a lady who was approximately 65 years old, came to me saying she was loving the seminars, but that not everything I had said applied to her, for her case was very different and the depression she experienced for years was due to her brain not producing serotonin, the happiness hormone. Then, she took out a plastic box full of serotonin pills imported from Germany. Looking at her bent posture, the drooped left shoulder, the head tilted down and to the side, I said that for her brain to have normal functions and produce the best possible chemistry, she would first have to change her body language, lifting her shoulders, her semblance, straightening her head, etc. She laughed as if nothing I was saying was making any sense, thanked me, and left.

Six days later, in the second part of the event, she reappeared, completely different. Her tone was vibrant, cheerful, enthusiastic, and she said she wanted to tell me all the changes that had happened to her. She told me that after her husband's death, her daughter had convinced her that she should take advantage of his retirement plan and stop working. Without her partner and an occupation, the daughter also convinced her she could no longer drive. And the next step was giving her daughter power of attorney to take care of her pension and retirement fund. At that point, she didn't have a husband, a job, freedom to come and go, and depended on her daughter's will to take her anywhere. She also didn't have any more money, for the daughter took all the income and disposed of it as she wished. The last stage was taking the mother to a psychiatrist; she must be depressed, since she was always sad, quiet, and crying her husband's death. How could a normal person not be depressed or at least melancholic living in that disguised prison? She had gotten to the seminar in that emotional state.

After our talk, she decided to try it for herself and see if what I had told her about posture was real. That same day she bought a posture-correcting brace and started using it. The next morning she already noticed changes in her attitude and her mood. In the second day she felt cheerier. In the fourth day, she rose from the ashes. The first thing she did was cancel her daughter's power of attorney and start collecting her pension and retirement fund herself. The second change was to get her car back from her daughter and to start driving again. With this, she was able to visit her sister and play cards again, which she hadn't done in years. The third big change was to accept the invitation from a friend to go to a weekly dance at the military club.

Her testimony was so strong that practically every student there cried, moved by her story. I asked: "Why did you put on that posture-correcting brace?" With a sly smile, she said: "Didn't you say that I had to change my body language for my brain to work well?" "Yes," I confirmed. "Well, after 65 years, 30 of them as a bank teller, it was hard for me to stand fully erect. So, when I put on the brace, everything got easier." She was applauded and hugged by her colleagues for the new life she had decided to conquer.

The problem was the next Monday, when this woman's daughter walked into my company in complete rage, accusing me of having destroyed her mother's life. Her mother was driving when she couldn't. Her mother was exposing herself in traffic coming and going from her friends' house, and she couldn't do that either, for she was old and senile. The result was that after the changes made by the mother, the daughter had to find a job and a place to live, since it didn't make much sense for a 38-year-old administrator to be supported by and live with her mother.

You can see how transforming it can be for anyone the simple act of regulating their non-verbal communication. Changes are immediate, and results are overwhelming. It is important for you to know that, the stronger your changes in non-verbal communication, the deeper, more consistent your gains will be. So, I would like for you to jump for joy right now, making plans to accomplish your most daring dreams. After all, what every experiment and research in Neuroscience show us is we can define our performance and our results just by regulating posture and non-verbal communication. How about adopting a high-performance linguistic style right now and revolutionizing your emotions and the way you face life? How about changing your non-verbal communication immediately and seeing yourself with the hands in the helm of your life?

EMOTIONAL ADDICTIONS

The same way the mouth reveals what the heart is full of, our posture exposes who we are. And for each posture or non-verbal communication we produce molecules of emotion—a chemical compound or combination of specific chemical compounds. These are neuropeptides or molecules of emotion, or chains of proteic amino acids produced by the hypothalamus. Crestfallen people with curved shoulders who look down systematically have specific molecules of emotion. Happy, lofty people who smile frequently, keep their shoulders straight, produce another pattern of molecules of emotion. If, right now, regardless of what is happening, you start to rant, fight, yell at the wall because you don't like the color it is painted, curse the floor for being flat, and complain about the clouds in the sky, your brain will obey that communication, as crazy as it is, and produce, among other compounds, adrenaline and cortisol, respectively, hormones responsible for anger and stress, in alarming, unnecessary amounts. And it won't produce serotonin, the happiness neurohormone, much less endorphin, the pleasure neurohormone. Behold a molecule of emotion produced by communication. It doesn't matter if communication is sensible, logical, beneficial or not, our organism will always produce the chemical correspondent to the communicated behavior. And the more intense or repeated it is, the more molecules will wander through your body and influence your life.

The same that happens with drugs also happens with the repeated use of the same molecule of emotion: receptors start to wait for—and even crave—that specific chemical. That means the body is dependent on the communication that produces that chemical. And believe me, your behavior and your attitude will be altered to obtain that chemical at any cost.

A friend who now lives in New Zealand sent me an e-mail telling me he thought he would die that year. I immediately called him to find out what was happening and how I could help him. During the talk, he confided in me: "I'm addicted." That sounded strange to me, because he had always been an athlete and had never drank or smoked. "What do you mean?" I asked. To which he answered: "You know that in Brazil I used to skydive, and, here in New Zealand I also do base jumping." He kept going: "So far, so good, the issue is that in base jumping, the goal is to be in free fall for the longest possible time and to open the parachute as close to the ground as possible. And the closer to the ground, the more adrenaline. I already broke my record six times this year." That was when he started to cry: "I lost two of my best friends to this sport and I think I'm next." I didn't understand, so I said: "Well, just open the parachute far from the ground." Still shaken-up, he explained: "You don't get it, I'm addicted to adrenaline and danger. I can't open my hand and release the parachute until I have the rush of adrenaline I need. It's an addiction. That's how Jenny and Mark died."

We started doing distance Systemic Integral Coaching and, in the process, he decided to have his first child. The day the baby was born, he quit the sport. Later, he told me something inside him had changed to the point that he was able to avoid the sport. Today, he tells everyone that oxytocin, the love hormone produced by his body with the birth of his child, saved his life.

Just like he was addicted to adrenalin and needed radical sports to feel satisfied, some people are addicted to trouble, they need problems and discussions to get "drunk" on the molecules of emotion. Others need victimization molecules of emotion and unconsciously create self-sabotaging situations. The fact is that to a lesser or larger extent; we are all addicted to something. The issue is knowing what to lean on and how to break the damaging cycle.

Next, I list the main emotional addictions I have found during these almost twenty years of career. As we know, each addiction is fueled by a specific linguistic pattern. I ask that you rate the intensity of each of those addictions in yourself, from 0 to 10. If your score is 0, it means you are not addicted to those molecules of emotion. From 5 up, you are starting to lose control, and after 8 you constantly create situations to be able to experience your addiction. You can broaden the list to include **unlisted addictions**. If you want, you can ask someone who knows you well to evaluate each of the addictions and think with you how addicted or not you are.

Emotional addictions
- Victimization ( )
- Anger ( )
- Problems ( )
- Stress ( )
- Control ( )
- Helping others ( )
- Constant activity/not allowing yourself to stop ( )
- Sadness ( )
- Illness ( )
- Loneliness ( )
- Abandonment ( )
- Being cheated or cheating ( )
- Being poor or in financial trouble ( )
- Always starting over ( )
- Being abused ( )
- Being ripped off or double-crossed ( )
- Fear ( )
- Pleasing others ( )
- Working and producing compulsively ( )
- Spending money ( )
- Sex ( )
- Lies ( )
- _____ ( )
- _____ ( )
- _____ ( )
- _____ ( )
- _____ ( )

In the following lines, list the five worst addictions you have identified in yourself. Then, identify losses and damages you experienced or have been experiencing because of this emotional/behavioral pattern.

Addiction 1: _____
Damage 1: _____
Damage 2: _____
Damage 3: _____

Addiction 2: _____
Damage 1: _____
Damage 2: _____
Damage 3: _____

Addiction 3: _____
Damage 1: _____
Damage 2: _____
Damage 3: _____

Addiction 4: _____
Damage 1: _____
Damage 2: _____
Damage 3: _____

Addiction 5: _____
Damage 1: _____
Damage 2: _____
Damage 3: _____

Now that you have identified the addictions that most sabotage your life, as well as the damages they cause, all is left is taking the next step to eliminate chemical dependence. How do you do that? By eliminating the emotional addictions.

ELIMINATING EMOTIONAL ADDICTIONS

Every human being, regardless of origin, race, schooling, culture, nationality, intelligence, age or genetics, has past addictions. Each addiction calls for a specific linguistic non-verbal communication or style, which, for its part, produces chemical addiction. Then the cycle begins again, and goes on continuously.

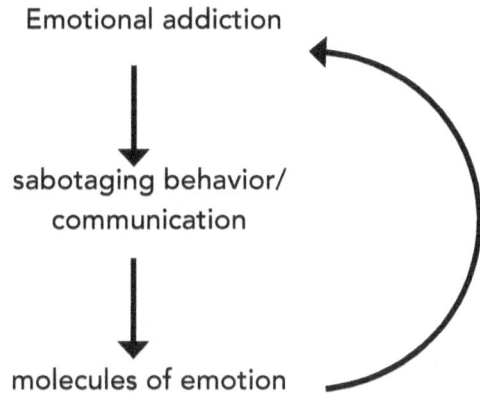

In CIS® Method, we have tools to interfere in many ways with this vicious cycle, among which are the linguistic styles and patterns that drastically alter your chemistry and addictions, about which we have talked in this chapter. Now, let's present an extremely powerful linguistic structure that, when repeated for the necessary period, will leave the brain long enough without the addictive chemical so that it gets cured by absence, and doesn't need molecules of emotion or sabotaging behaviors anymore.

As you already know, every behavior carries molecules of emotion with it, and our brain gets addicted to these molecules. If you are addicted to stress, you need a specific verbal behavior, like frowning, pacing around with your head down, biting your lips etc., which, in turn, will produce high levels of cortisol. If you are addicted to depression and sadness, you will also have a specific linguistic style, with arched shoulders, downward gaze with a drooped brow, head tilting to the side, and the brain will produce the specific molecules of emotion.

Our goal here is to establish specific linguistic exercises capable of producing a compound strong enough to fight all emotional addictions at the same time, whatever they are. And what I can say is, to our surprise, this strategy has not only successfully combated the emotional addiction symptoms but also had extraordinary results in fighting addiction to legal and illegal drugs.

To give you a good measure, we have an average of 10 to 15 people in every CIS® Method that decide to quit drugs and, of those, 90% stay on the wagon throughout the time. Obviously, a lot of these things happen during the CIS® Method, and surely postural communication exercises make all the difference.

No human being can go without feeling some kind of emotion at every possible moment, so, what we will do is to substitute bad, sabotaging emotions with positive, strengthening ones. Therefore, we will intensely and repeatedly communicate non-verbal linguistic exercises capable of producing five emotions, which we will call primary curative emotions (PCE): power, victory, peace, joy/enthusiasm, and love. I want to state again that the idea is to constantly generate new patterns for molecules of emotion, so that in very little time the abstinent body forgets the molecules of past addictions and we start to display new behaviors, new feelings, and new life results.

As the Harvard researcher and psychologist Amy Cuddy says, non-verbal body language necessarily shapes and reinforces who we are. This means we are free to change our identity beliefs as we repeatedly and intensely present a new communication. Our minds will search for congruence with this new behavior/communication and, starting from that, will shape our whole beings, regulating a new identity that looks like our new ways of acting, speaking, and maintain our postures.

For the linguistic exercises to have a real impact, two rules will have to be followed: 1- they will have to be done repeatedly throughout a period of time; 2- and under heavy emotional impact. To repeat it throughout a period of time, all you have to do is create a daily schedule and systematically repeat it for days and weeks. As to do it under heavy emotional impact, you will need to use your whole body in an exaggerated/intense way to communicate each of the primary curative emotions. I usually train my students by yelling this mantra very loudly dozens of times: "Emotion lodges in the flesh; emotion lodges in the flesh...". We do this bending our knees, looking up, and clapping our hands on our bodies. All of this is to develop the emotion needed to produce the molecules of emotion we want.

A great international coach, Tony Robbins, says: "Motion is emotion," meaning that moving the body produces emotion. So, the more intense the non-verbal communication, the more emotions are produced.

Next, I list the six primary curative feelings produced by each type of communication, the main hormones or neurohormones produced by this communication and, lastly, the posture to imitate, with a drawing pertaining to each PCE.

FIRST PATTERN: POWER

Scientist Amy Cuddy demonstrates in her experiences that staying for just two minutes in the *power position* commonly used by Wonder Woman—open shoulders, head pointing to the horizon—raises testosterone levels by 20%. With increased testosterone levels, the feelings of control and dominance surge immediately. As a consequence of the perceived power, cortisol levels, the stress hormone, drops about 15%.

It seems magical to be able to alter our perception of the world and leave behind a state of no power, gaining dominance and control in a matter of seconds. But adopting the opposite posture, that is, looking down, tightening the eyes, curving the shoulders, crossing the arms, and becoming small, we immediately have a chemical alteration and new molecules of emotion arise. This time, however, the molecules will make a person sad, unmotivated, insecure, and impotent. And all this is due to non-verbal communication. It is freeing, hopeful, and curative to be able to choose what you want to communicate and, by systematically repeating this communication, become emotionally equal to practiced communication.

So, if you are a bit more restrained, you can just hold the power position for two minutes. However, if you want deeper, faster, transforming results, you can do the second power exercise according to the following sequence of illustrations:

SECOND PATTERN: VICTORY

When you communicate sadness, your body immediately produces sadness molecules of emotion, a combination of hormones and neurohormones that includes lower production of serotonin, less dopamine, less testosterones, and more cortisol, besides an exaggerated or inconsistent production of noradrenaline.

However, when you communicate victory in deeds, words, and actions, a new biochemical production takes place and inundates the whole central nervous system, producing a drastic change in perception, action, and reaction to the environment. The proposal here is to vigorously send stimuli (communication) of victory to the brain, so that it produces or orders the production of victory molecules of emotion to fight the feeling of sadness, apathy and despondency.

The victory pose, like in the drawing, is universal. Social scientist Jessica Tracy, from the University of British Columbia, has demonstrated that even people who are born blind use the same posture: arms up in a V-shape, open chest, and chin pointed upwards. This discovery proves there are instinctive non-verbal communications, natural to all human beings. We can (and should) use them to shape our new planned identity.

THIRD PATTERN: HAPPINESS

To produce this pattern, it is essential to first differentiate happiness from joy. Whereas the first is directly linked to momentary, fleeting pleasure, the second is connected to a state of contentment, through combined feelings of peace, faith, and love.

A few years ago, when I stopped racing 4x4, my rally partner asked me: "Paulo, how can you always feel so good? I keep racing cars, I do jiu-jitsu, I have my cards party, I play soccer twice a week, not to mention the parties—I go to all of them. And I'm always feeling down and depressed. You, on the other hand, don't do half of that and are always well. How is that?" I answered: "Friend, you keep searching for joy, and I search for happiness. You have been basing your life on fleeting things, I base mine on permanent ones. You invest your time and focus in getting, and I focus a good deal on getting and also giving. And believe me, giving is always better."

Another acquaintance confided in me after receiving an almost billionaire inheritance, saying happiness is the sum of all the moments of joy. After his explanation, I couldn't help asking: "Are you honestly happy with all that money and a life dedicated to pleasure?" "What do you mean?" he wanted to know. I explained: "Today, you have the most beautiful women at your disposal. You travel to the most beautiful places in the world. You take weekly motorcycle trips with your group. You taste cigars and rare wines in your cinematic home every week. Do you honestly feel happy after all that?" He looked down and up. He tried to hold back tears. And then he said: "No,

I'm not. I think I search for all that agitation and pleasure, so I don't have to look at myself and who I am." I am not saying joy is not important, because it is. But you need to know how to produce a feeling of happiness through linguistic patterns and styles and through the communication of peace, faith, and love.

Given the broadness of happiness, we will combine a non-verbal exercise with all that you have learned about gratitude and the perfect language. Let's see the linguistic pattern of happiness:

1º) Daily 40-second hugs in people who are important in your life, with whom you have family bonds or true alliances. Notice this exercise is about giving love, not receiving.

2º) Validation: this exercise breaks the uniquely non-verbal pattern and combines a semblance of acceptance and love with a verbal compliment, given with a smile. For the effect to be overwhelming and fast, you need to repeat it ten times a day with every person you can possibly compliment. It could be anyone, the important thing is for this communication to be as strong and intense as possible and in fact make a difference to the receiver. Once again, it is an act of giving, not receiving.

3º) This exercise is based on shouting "Yes!" for joy 30 times over. The following drawing shows the movement of the arms and the final position.

4º) Manifesting gratitude as a linguistic style, as previously explained in this chapter.

Those who fear ridicule never get close to the extraordinary. A lot of people will try these exercises, feel fake, childish, silly, and stop right after. If you try the proposed exercises and feel that way, I ask that you reflect on your life and think whether the fear of ridicule has stopped you from accomplishing so much more. Is it worth it to save face when the price to pay is so high?

Pay attention to the fable called *The old man, the boy, and the donkey*. Notice that, no matter our attitude, there will always be someone to complain about our choices.

Once upon a time, an old man decided to teach his grandson to lead a little donkey the family owned. Full of happiness, a certain morning, the grandfather prepared the animal's saddle, called the child, and told him he would learn to lead the donkey that day.

The grandson then led the donkey by holding the harness, while the grandfather happily and proudly rode the animal and watched him. Suddenly, a group of people passed by and said:

"That's absurd! That poor boy leading the donkey and the old man riding... So awful!"

Embarrassed because they were badmouthing him, the grandfather decided to put his grandson on the donkey and lead the animal himself. So, he continued on this path, while the grandson, riding the donkey, was happy and proud to see his grandfather walking beside him.

They heard another group commenting:

"That's absurd! While the boy rides the donkey, the poor old man walks..."

Mortified with what they were thinking about his grandson, the grandfather took him off the donkey and they both walked, hand in hand.

When they got to town, another group passed them by, saying:

"That's absurd! The old man and the boy walking and no one riding the donkey. So many people in need of an animal, they should give it to those who need it."

The grandfather looked at those people and, at a loss of what to do, rode the donkey with the grandson, believing he would finally make everyone happy. But other people passed them by, saying:

"That's absurd! Two people riding a donkey, they'll break the poor animal's back!"

The grandfather then realized that, no matter what you do, someone will always have something bad to say.

I have been challenging people to manifest depression with those exercises. I have never seen anyone complain about depression and, at the same time, compliment the people around them positively. I have never heard depressive people say: "I am grateful for your life, you make a difference." I have never seen people shout for joy, strongly and intensely, but still feel beaten down and unmotivated. It might not be easy for those in a profound state of depression to change their communication pattern and adopt this new language. However, be it with self-determination, the help of people who are close to them, the motivation and dynamic of a seminar, be it with the help of medication, I have seen people break free of this prison. I have seen people who had been taking controlled medicine for over 15 years have them suspended by their doctors, stunned in realizing their patient didn't need prescriptions anymore.

FOURTH PATTERN: JOY AND ENTHUSIASM

This pattern also makes a lot of difference in human psyche. After all, when we communicate intense joy, our brains start producing and balancing the neurohormone called endorphin, which stimulates short-term memory, alleviates physical and emotional pains, not to mention giving the sensation of joy and well-being. The linguistic exercise proposed here can be the same natural behavior or communication displayed by a sports fan when his team wins an important championship. Or by someone who wins a huge lottery prize. In moments like these, functional people celebrate the win with a very high emotional intensity. And that is exactly what I propose here: that you stop and, for thirty seconds, communicate an intense celebration, it doesn't matter what for. Just celebrate intensely and feel what has changed inside you.

FIFTH PATTERN: PEACE

Cerebral waves are electromagnetic waves produced by neuron activity. They change frequency based on neuron's electric activity; this is related to changes in states of consciousness (excitement, concentration, relaxation, meditation, transcendence, etc.). In a high-activity pattern, our cerebral wave frequency is high. The idea now is to change that, relax a little and slow down.

In the peace pattern, you get up and straighten your body, relaxing your face and shoulders without letting them drop, close your eyes, and repeat from 20 to 30 times the word "peace," elongating the "c" sound. Knowing the modern lifestyle, we can stop at any calm, private place throughout the day to lower our cerebral frequency and get good results. Follow the illustration to reproduce the linguistic pattern of peace.

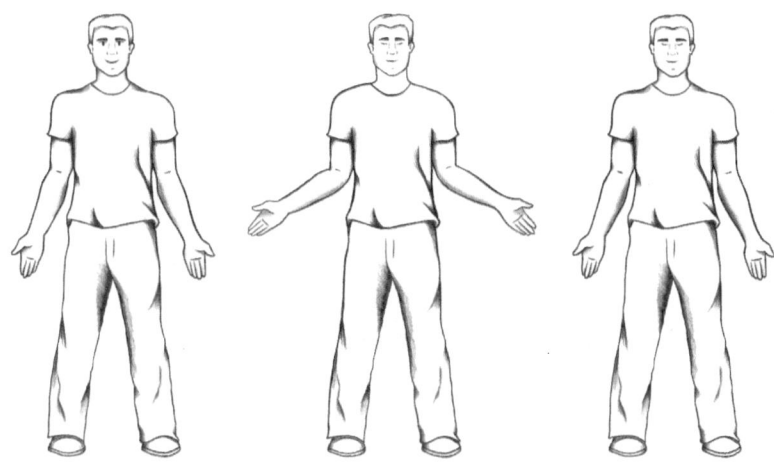

SIXTH PATTERN: LOVE

In the old days, oxytocin was known simply as the *love hormone*. Today, with advances in Neuroscience, it is also called the *social connection hormone*. It is responsible for creating social and affectionate bonds. In women, it is also responsible for pre- and post-partum uterine contraction. In post-partum, every time the baby sucks milk from the mother's breast, the hypothalamus and the uterus itself produce high doses of oxytocin, which not only contract the uterus, helping it to return to its natural state, but also create a strong mother-child bond. Among other benefits, oxytocin fights aggressiveness produced by testosterone and diminishes the amount of cortisol in the body. Currently, there are two topics related to oxytocin that are being studied: its impact on fidelity and obesity.

As far as fidelity, a study done at Bonn University by neuroscientist Rene Hurlemann with 40 heterosexual men suggests high doses of oxytocin produce marital fidelity through a greater positive emotional connection between the man and his partner. The second benefit studied is the hormone's effect on reward systems: an amount of oxytocin in the blood substitutes other types of behavioral rewards such as drugs, shopping, food, sugar, etc. This means if a person produces enough oxytocin, they should be able to refrain the impulse for shopping, drugs, and food. In 2013, Yale University published a scientific paper showing oxytocin is strongly related to socialization in children with autism.

The question is: how can we produce this emotional elixir? To have oxytocin in a curative amount, we need non-verbal and verbal communication of self-love and love for those closest to us, like family, relatives, and close friends. We also need to treat well or very well anyone who crosses our path, so emotional chemistry isn't undone. Let me remind you that indifference or non-perception of others is already a negative communication and, like any feeling, will produce its pertinent molecules of emotion.

We can get oxytocin with the 40-second hug, constant validation, and, especially, physical and verbal affection in a peaceful state. This means that, when we dedicate ourselves to the exercises to conquer the other five patterns, this sixth one—love—comes as a consequence of wonderful benefits for your life. It is like an award for attaining a goal for which you have worked with such disposition and strength.

We have just seen six emotional patterns created by verbal and non-verbal communication styles. It is important that you open up to what is scientific and to change possibilities that go beyond controlled medicine and other traditional cognitive-behavioral treatments.

These are six primary curative emotional patterns that anyone can exercise anytime and anywhere that is minimally appropriate. The issues are with what emotional weight and with what frequency will you do your curative emotional exercises to eliminate addictions that have imprisoned you and limited you in many areas of life. The first question might be: "Will you do these exercises tested by Harvard and Yale researchers today to change your life or will you tell tales to justify why you are not doing the exercises and keep living the same life and being the same person?" If that is your attitude, I can say to you what I have been saying to many people: "Don't worry. It's alright. Everyone has the life they deserve." If you are willing to pay the price only you can pay, let's get to it, for there is a lot of work to be done and it is time to get started.

HOW TO PRACTICE THE PATTERNS

Our observation and empirical modelling come from hundreds and hundreds of clients, both in individual coaching and the CIS® Method Seminar. The approach to exercise communication is based on three premises detailed below: necessity, intensity, and repetition.

NECESSITY

You have learned six linguistic patterns and their biochemical effects on humans. Now, you need, by your own observation or other people's feedback, to recognize what your addictions are and practice the exercises most suited for your case. If you are addicted to stress, the patterns to practice most are certainly the peace and power ones. With the relaxation created by alpha waves, the feeling of peace comes immediately; with the shout and the movements of power, testosterone is produced and brings a sensation of control and dominance.

Don't forget, however, that in the end of the day, those exercises must be brought into your daily life as a linguistic style and a lifestyle. For more benefits, you should ideally practice all the patterns, always emphasizing those you need the most.

INTENSITY

As you already know, emotion lodges in the flesh, and for an effective reprogramming of beliefs and a quick elimination of addictions, you should consider that the cognitive and intellectual side has only a 15% influence over our deep emotional changes. Therefore, emotional intensity will make all the difference in eliminating your addictions.

Therefore I suggest you dedicate yourself entirely to the proposed exercises. Don't be ashamed or afraid to show, in your gestures and posture, what you want for yourself, even if it sounds ridiculous. Act with intensity, making big, strong gestures. The more you use the body movements, the faster and deeper changes will take place, and more long-lasting they will be.

REPETITION

The intensity you put into the exercises is important, but not enough to get the desired results. We can compare it to the physical activity of lifting weights. While the weight lifted is extremely important, it is the repetition that will truly strengthen the muscle.

Therefore, for the proposed linguistic exercises to heal emotional addictions, what will make the difference is the amount of times you repeat them throughout the day. If you are looking for real results, you need to not only apply emotional intensity, but also to do each exercise at least five times a day, with 20 to 30 repetitions each time.

ABOUT STRESS

Unlike many other academic fields, Neuroscience has no rein or boundary. It continually launches multidirectional theses and possibilities that sometimes go against old certainties and unquestionable beliefs. In an article entitled "Depressão e estresse" [Depression and Stress], Brazilian doctor Drauzio Varella presents a debate published in *Science* magazine about the currently most accepted set of ideas to explain depression: the stress hypothesis.

According to that hypothesis, the hypothalamus produces a hormone (CRF) as a reaction to aggressive stimuli in an environment, to try and convince the hypophysis to order the adrenal glands to produce cortisol and other end-products of cortisone. Their job is to generate extra care and attention.

Several experimental works have showed these stress hormones (cortisol and other derived hormones) are prejudicial to neuron health, because they modify the chemical composition of the medium in which these cells work. The persistence of stress, and consequently of cortisol, alters the neuronal circuits' architecture in such a way as to change the very anatomy of the brain. For example, it reduces the dimensions of the hippocampus, a structure involved with memory, essential for anti-depressive medication to work. This could explain Alzheimer's and other neural illnesses.

Researchers from the University of Emory, Atlanta, have demonstrated that critical experiences in childhood, such as physical violence, sexual abuse, not being cared or loved by one's mother, and other types of emotional stress, can lead the hypothalamus to hyper-secrete CFR, consequently making adrenal glands release cortisol. These alterations are associated with depression and other emotional dysfunctions in adult life. Researchers have concluded that many of the neurobiochemical alterations found in adult depression can be explained by stress undergone in early phases of childhood.

I will approach this subject in more depth in Chapter VII, about beliefs, when I draw attention to the quality and intensity of your communication with your children. I will advocate for direct communication, which is related to what you explicitly and directly say or demonstrate; and also to indirect communication, which your children don't get from what you do, but from what you don't do and the environment you put them in. Remember: what you communicate—or don't communicate—to your children will echo through eternity.

CHAPTER VI
QUESTION

Your mind will answer all your questions, but first you must ask them truly. Then, just relax, for the answers will come.
(Paulo Vieira)

After so many setbacks in my life, from 17 to 30, I found out that what hurt me the most during that painful time wasn't what I didn't know, but what I knew. I had so many truths and certainties inside me that there simply wasn't any room to learn or experience anything that hadn't been pre-programmed in my mind. In my case, it is like my HD was full of inefficient programs and I wasn't freeing space for other, better-quality ones. When we talk about the human mind, freeing space would be enough for new information and knowledge to be absorbed, even if by osmosis. However, for over thirteen years I clung to my truths, defending them with such passion that few would dare dissuade me. When I found people truly willing to do it, they were just like me, stuck and chained to their absolute truths, so we would enter in humongous fights, each wanting to defend their own point of view. Such time lost, such pain felt, so many dreams shattered by the walls of absolute truths.

Knowing how to ask questions is much more important than knowing how to ask for things. How many women have asked for a husband and, when he came, they lived the most miserable days of their lives. How many people have asked for wealth and, when it came, happiness and peace of mind were gone? How many young people have asked for a car and lost their lives inside of it?

Knowing how to ask the right questions gives direction to our desires and gets us to ask what is truly beneficial. Good questions will invariably show us paths, but only the best questions will show us the purposes and values behind what we want and how we think about accomplishing it.

Answers will always be important, but they are not superior to questions in importance and power. For answers are usually limited and time-based, while questions are unlimited and timeless.
(Paulo Vieira)

I was at a christening reception watching my son and other children playing Tarzan, jumping on everything around them, when one of the parents yelled loudly at his young 4-year old and, along with the yelling, came adjectives and threats of beating. Since the older children kept jumping, the kid who had been reprimanded stayed aside watching his friends jump heroically over the abyss, with a sad gaze and hunched posture.

The yell was so loud, aggressive, and humiliating that I couldn't help but, as the father, ask: "I'm sorry to interfere, but what was your goal in scolding your son like that?" And he answered: "Well, the goal was to get him to stop jumping." I said: "If that was your only goal, you achieved it. Congratulations. Your child is there all hunched up, looking at the other children jump." But I continued: "Now, if your goal is to have an emotionally healthy, strong, determined child, you should question the education you're giving him. What you're getting from this type of education is to destroy your son's self-esteem. And one thing I know: in the future, he will need people to yell at him in some moments and, in others, he will look for weaker people to mistreat, like you're doing to him now. He will surely mistreat those he loves and be mistreated by outsiders. This is what you're getting." He said: "I never stopped to think of it like that."

This is the problem: people don't stop to think why they act, how they act, or why they want what they want. It's time to start questioning a lot in your life, while there is time.

QUALIFYING THE QUESTIONS

If we qualify people by their questions, the first, most elemental level would be made up of those who don't ask any, sometimes accepting other people's truths; sometimes guiding themselves by their own. For instance: "This is the best job for you!" "You have to study Medicine." "You will only be happy if you marry so-and-so." In this first level, people only listen, without questioning.

I am not saying your truths or other people's truths are good or bad. I am just questioning whether they are valid for your present moment. After all, answers are essential, but they are not superior to questions in importance and power. For answers are usually limited and time-based, while questions are the exact opposite. When someone tells you what to do, be open to three things: completely accepting it, completely rejecting it, or accepting one part and rejecting the rest. To make this decision, you need to ask more and more questions:

1a) Is this person's advice what is best for me?
1b) Is what I want in fact what is best for me?
2a) Is what they want me to do appropriate to my life's context? Maybe they don't know my fears, my insecurities, my ambitions, and my desires.
2b) Is what I want to do appropriate to my life's context? Is it appropriate considering my fears, my insecurities, my ambitions, and my desires?
3a) Is what they are telling me to do part of my beliefs and personal values?

3b) Is what I am thinking of doing part of my beliefs and personal values?
4a) Even if that person is right and this is the best choice, am I ready today to do what they want me to do?
4b) Even if I am sure and this is the best choice, am I ready today to do it?
5a) Even if I do what this person wants me to do, will I be happy doing it? Is that what I was born to do?
5b) Even if I do what seems best, will I be happy doing it? Is that what I was born to do?

Victorious people search a multitude of advisers. Emotionally limited people, on the other hand, search their path and destiny alone, never questioning it. When we hear our truth and other people's truth, we need to keep two questions in mind: Who is the person we are listening to? What results have they been experiencing? It is common sense to first have faith in the intention of our adviser and, then, in the person's competence in that area. It might not be as fruitful or safe to ask my grandfather for advice about financial investments if he never prospered in that. Even if I hear what he has to say, I need to hear a lot of other people. Especially, I need to question all of them and their truths, including myself and my truth. This can be done with the following questions:

1. Do I or does that person have experience in that aspect of life?
2. Do I or does that person have practical results that validate each of our ideas?
3. Am I or is that person saying what I want to hear to make me happy, or are we saying what in fact is best for me in the long run?
4. Do I or does that person have emotional and intellectual maturity in that specific aspect of life?

If in the basis of the human evolutionary pyramid, the most elemental level are people who don't question, in the second tier are people who question, but in the worst possible way: they ask little and, when they do, the questions weaken and debilitate them. They question things like:

- Why did this happen to me?
- Did I deserve this?
- Will I be able to accomplish this dream?
- Will I make money out of it?

These are questions that carry answers within them, but answers that put the person in a worse situation than before. These types of questions don't generate action or focus on the future, instead, they bring only doubt and fear.

The third group of people are those who ask good questions and, therefore, get good answers. They ask about what they want, what they should do, and how they can do it. These are much more evolved, consistent questions, and so they are ahead of most people around them. They question, and that matters. These people know how to stop and plan focused, efficient actions. They ask questions like:

- What is our next step?
- How will we achieve our goals?
- Who will be part of the team?
- What do we really want to accomplish?
- What is the way forward?
- What resources do we need to get there?

However, not even these people are on the top of the emotional maturity pyramid, because they focus only on the path (how) and the destination (what or where), but don't know exactly why they tread that path or the reason why that goal is the best one.

True super-humans know how to question themselves to the point of figuring out their purposes and whys. They find out their personal values and life mission, which are behind what they think, feel, and do. They discover a source of endless fuel which will get them to where ordinary people don't even dream of. These people leave a legacy on Earth.

They ask constant PQWs and this gets them to the heart of the matter. These are questions like:

1. What is the purpose of the education and love I am giving my children?
2. What is in fact a happy, prosperous home?
3. What is the bigger purpose in marrying this person?
4. What is the bigger purpose in working with this?
5. What keeps me working in my father's company?
6. What does life have to offer me that I still have to see?

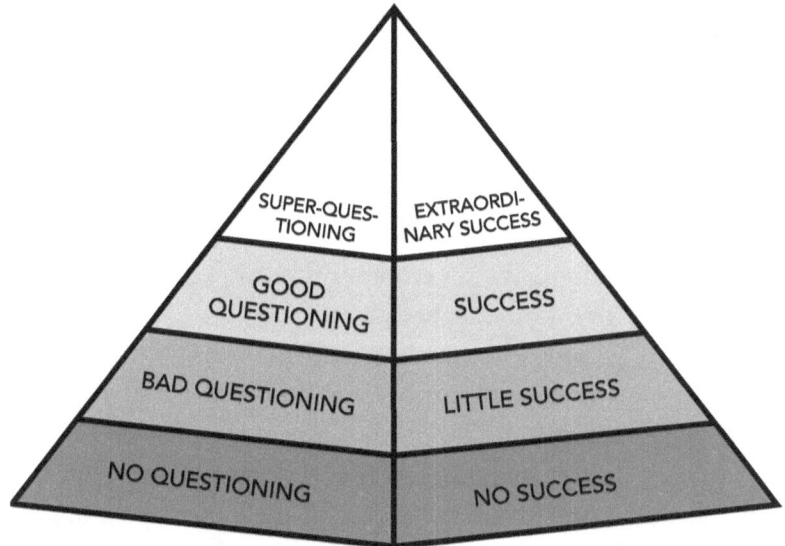

A friend of my wife's family started asking questions about her life. She felt confused, sad, and didn't know what was wrong. Intuitively, she started asking herself questions. Then, she started writing down the best questions. After a week, she had over 30 questions, just questions. Since nothing happens by chance, a person who had taken the CIS® Method suddenly appeared and started talking about the experiences and changes after the event. She felt like God was telling her that her questions, too, had answers. She and her husband took the course. Changes were immediate and are still happening. The husband was a good father and became an even better one. The marriage was peaceful and became even better. The husband's engineering company, who had for two years had a rope around its neck, always on the edge, recently made in one month 20% more than in the whole year before. A lot more things happened in every area of that family's life. The answer she got was a question I always ask in the beginning of my seminar:

> *Why keep being the same person as always if you can be someone much better?*
> (Richard Bandler)

This question was enough for her to understand she was living in the same-old mediocrity zone and that she and her husband were comfortably seated on top of the cask, in the comfort zone. There, in the first hours of the seminar, the penny dropped and their motto became: CHANGE NOW! As she asked and answered more questions, other actions, decisions, changes, and beliefs came into play. In very little time, what once was a truth completely tumbled and gave way to confusion. After confusion, however, came a new reality, one of abundance and prosperity.

I see a lot of people who demand study and good grades from their children, with such severity that it bothers me. When someone does that, I ask them why such weight on grades and performance. They quickly answer: "So they can be successful in life." I reply with another question: "And what is success for your son in the future?" Most people get lost at that point. Some say it is professional stability, others say financial independency, others say being happy. I retort: "What is professional stability? What is financial independency? What is happiness for your children in the future? And is it in fact what is most important for them?" Again, confused answers arise.

What happens to these people is they haven't stopped for a moment to question their way of educating and loving their children, much less to learn what they really want, and why they want that future for themselves. Good grades matter, it is true, but beyond that, what is most important for your son's future—and to which you are not paying due attention? Do you know anyone who succeeded in life without getting such good grades? How much in terms of value and principles have you been striving to pass on to your children? And what about the emotional aspect? Have you filled your kids with warm moments so as to make them strong and daring in the future?

This is the line of thought of those who have an abundant life. If your life isn't abundant, it is because there is a dysfunction, and all dysfunctions can and should be questioned and, then, eliminated. For that, we must constantly ask the Powerful Questions of Wisdom (PQW) which we will address next.

POWERFUL WISDOM QUESTIONS

Super-human people ask Powerful Questions of Wisdom (PQW) as a form of abundant lifestyle. These people question their limits, their origins, and their fears; they question everything that could somehow be better. They even question their accomplishments and victories. For a super-human, however, knowing how to question is not enough; they must search for the answers to their questions. An answer will never be enough by itself.

Each man must be aware that his mission is to live a life full of meaning, and respond with self-transcendence to every situation. For more people today have the means to live, but no meaning to live for. (Viktor Frankl)

Martin Luther King is a perfect example of someone who became super-human by questioning the United States' and the world's truths. Coming from a Baptist family, he grew up as a young questioner, to the point that at the age of 13, at the Sunday school of the church attended by his family, he questioned Christ's bodily resurrection. Amidst the controversy and confusion caused by his questionings, he declared: "Doubts started to inexorably arise."

Later, then, he said the *Bible* had a lot of inescapable deep truths. Still young, he entered a Theology seminar and graduated as the most prominent black reverend of all time. But he didn't stop questioning established truths, becoming the person who peacefully mobilized the world against

North-American segregation and racial prejudice. With his speeches, like the famous "I have a Dream," he crossed America back to back, making people question the truths about the country's racial situation. The United States changed their law, their way of being and acting towards all people regardless of race or culture. All this because he decided to question current truths. And King didn't stop there: among other subjects, starting in 1965, he started questioning the United States' intentions in the Vietnam War.

Someone else who decided to question what was being accepted as true was Nick Vujicic. He was born with no arms or legs due to Tetra-amelia syndrome. At 8 years of age, he thought about suicide, not only because of the natural limitations of his physical condition, but also because of being bullied at school. At 16, however, he started to question his limitations and later opened his own non-profit organization, called Life Without Limbs.

At 21, he graduated in Accounting and Finances. Since then, he has been traveling the world to talk about hope and faith. He questions his limitations and asks himself: "Would I be here with you guys if not for my disability? So, what is limitation if not what we believe it is?" Another super-human asking the right questions and, as from there, creating a world of possibilities.

> *Everything can be taken from a man, but one thing: the last of the human freedoms—to choose one's attitude in any given set of circumstances, to choose one's own way.*
> (Viktor Frankl)

Looking at your life, I ask you to identify your limitations. What are your difficulties or what could simply be better in your life?

Now, I want you to question the things that are really very bad in your life or around you, as well as the things that could simply be better, but you hadn't stopped to question them or act differently. Select five realities and write them down below.

1. _____
2. _____
3. _____
4. _____
5. _____

Be aware of the fact that super-humans don't look for shortcuts to their questions, nor do they search for the easiest answers. They look for what is truly better. Think about Martin Luther King; he could have gone into armed struggle, but he didn't. He always led peaceful marches, with the goal not to destroy, but to build a society with new possibilities. The same is true of other super-questioners, like Gandhi and Nelson Mandela. Their questions didn't lead them to revolutions, in the sense of harsh or violent destruction, but to building and evolving. If your questions lead you to destroy what you have, it is time to question your questions and your answers.

But what distinguishes common questions from PQWs? Here follow five criteria:

1°) Mainly future-oriented.
2°) Action- and reflection-oriented.
3°) Solution-oriented.
4°) Goal-oriented.
5°) Self-accountability-oriented.

For a question about your life to be good, you need to follow the five criteria and, to verify the quality of your PQW, you can compare it to the following orientation:

Powerful Questions of Wisdom…
- … make me think and rethink.
- … produce good answers.
- … produce real action.

- ... generate new possibilities.
- ... create space for flexibility.
- ... offer powerful answers and solutions.

Powerful questions generate bountifulness and life abundance. If you are not experiencing tremendous positive results, it is because you are imprisoned in the basis of the questioning-types pyramid. Go to it and sincerely place your level of emotional maturity in questioning current reality.

Return to the five realities you listed in the last exercise. How about you start asking at least ten powerful questions for each of them, according to the following example?

General questioning: my financial life is precarious, limited, and indebted.
1st **PQW:** who says I have to spend my life around financial problems?
2nd **PQW:** is there someone who was like me financially and turned it around shortly?
3rd **PQW:** what do I need to do differently to prosper financially, increasing my income by 50%?
4th **PQW:** what do I need to learn to prosper financially?
5th **PQW:** what will I do and how will I act to end my overdraft?
6th **PQW:** who will I become when I am truly rich?
7th **PQW:** with what will I work to make 5 million?
8th **PQW:** who are the people that are with me on this journey?
9th **PQW:** what price am I willing to pay for financial success?
10th **PQW:** how will I pay back God and the world for my future financial achievements?

The PQWs don't need to be perfect, and you don't need to be a master in the art of questioning. In this first moment, the goal is not necessarily to build a bridge from where you were to where you want to go, but to destroy the emotional walls that kept you from seeing other possibilities and pointing to a new vision and a new way of acting, thinking, and feeling.

EXERCISE

From the example given, write what needs to be questioned in your life and then ask PQWs to tear down the walls of impossibility. You can do the exercise for all the areas of your life you think interesting to reassess.

General questioning: _____
1st PQW: _____
2nd PQW: _____
3rd PQW: _____
4th PQW: _____
5th PQW: _____
6th PQW: _____
7th PQW: _____
8th PQW: _____
9th PQW: _____
10th PQW: _____

> *Limited people ask if they will make it, winning people ask what they will do to make it. And super-humans ask who they will become when they make it.*
> (Paulo Vieira)

SELF-COACHING

Helping so many people with CIS and in part thanks to the PQWs, I decided to be the test subject of my own experiments. It was 2006, I was on a flight from Fortaleza to São Paulo, bothered by the flow of trips I had to make for lectures and seminars. At that time, I spent an average of ten to fifteen days away from my house, and hugely missed my wife and 3-year-old girl. Not to mention that in October of that year I would have my second son. The fact was, I didn't want to spend so much time away from home anymore. So, for the first time, I did what I called self-coaching. My goal was to double what I made for each coaching session. In three months, I went from 500 reais per session to 1,000. That answered the most important of my questions: How will I travel less to minister lectures and seminars, and have more time at home with my children without lowering my standard of living? Then, I understood once and for all that questions were answers, and answers were transforming my reality at an unbelievable speed.

I liked the first round and went to the second. This time, I wasn't only charging 1,500 reais per session, but also having 20 active weekly clients. Again, a world of surprising actions, plans, and events took place: 21 active clients, all paying around 1,500. Then I did it for the third time before the end of the year, and again experienced more changes and extraordinary gains. At that time, I had over 25 active clients paying around 2,000 per session. The fact that I started the year charging 500 and ended it obtaining four times more was just amazing.

Since 2006, self-coaching has been a constant in my life and, when people ask me how a small coaching institute managed to become the largest in Latin America and be among the top two or three in the world in such short time, the answer is simple: self-coaching. It is about questioning possibilities as a lifestyle. It is about asking yourself every day: "Why not?"

It is a deep process that uses PQWs, usually focused on a specific, viewable, time-based, challenging goal. The purpose of this exercise is to promote self-accountability, clearness of purposes, and a package of consistent actions and decisions towards the goal. As you already know, those who act have power, and those who act right have even more power. Self-coaching should be used in the search for challenging goals and solutions for problems, and can go from super-specific objectives to more generic ones. For instance, it can go from how to increase your salary to how to be happy, fulfilled, and accomplished in your life. In both cases, what is important is that you can visualize it.

STAGES OF SELF-COACHING

To understand how to apply self-coaching, I will use the example of a person who wants to earn a 15,000-monthly wage. The process has nine steps:

1st **step**: Define the goal. In this case, getting a monthly revenue of 15,000.
2nd **step**: Be sure that the set goal is viewable.
3rd **step**: List 35 questions such as how, which, when, what, where, why, in what way, and so on, always repeating the goal. Examples:
- What will I change in my behavior within the company to earn a 15,000-monthly wage?
- What will I study and learn to earn a 15,000-monthly wage?
- Who will I get close to inside and outside the company to earn a 15,000-monthly wage?
- What mistakes will I stop making to earn a 15,000-monthly wage?

4th **step**: after listing the 35 focal questions, close the notebook and spend two to three days without thinking about the questions or the intended goal.
5th **step**: after the two-day pause, answer the 35 questions with rich details and commitment.
6th **step**: put the answers in order of priority and execution, eliminating the ones that are not suitable.
7th **step**: after organizing and eliminating the irrelevant ones, print the relevant answers, transforming them in an informal action plan.
8th **step**: read your answers/action plan every day and immediately schedule, execute and finish each of the tasks.
9th **step**: even if it doesn't make sense, read all your self-coaching questions out loud, if possible.

After that, answers will start to arise and, with them, drastic changes will come.

Now that you have this powerful tool, what will you do with it? Leave is a theoretical contemplation while others change their lives? Tell tales to justify not using it? Or follow up with an endless journey of conquests? You are free to make your decisions, and always will be. I hope, however, you have convinced yourself you can have an abundant life now, and quicker than you imagined.

CHAPTER VII
BELIEVE

But when you ask, you must believe and not doubt, because the one who doubts is like a wave of the sea, blown and tossed by the wind. ... Such a person is double-minded and unstable in all they do.
(James 1:6 and James 1:8)

A lot of people wonder why they are poor or sad, and the easiest and simplest answer is to blame their parents, the environment in which they live, or even the government. However, we frequently see people in poor environments who become rich. And we see people who are happy despite living in great adversity. In this chapter, I want to present another possibility for our results and lifestyle: our beliefs. And when I say belief, I don't mean religious creed, but a mental programming in the form of **neural circuits**, a vast, extensive network of neurons connected to millions of other neurons. These circuits carry information or programs that govern and command all human behaviors and reactions to stimuli. The neural circuits storage all learning, and information accumulated by someone throughout his life, and even in the womb. All of this is stored in the conscious mind and in the unconscious, structured both in the left side and the right side of the brain.

Through these circuits or neural networks, the brain can produce responses for each internal or external stimulus, as well as the behaviors and attitudes of a person towards life. Every living being has an organized, interconnected nervous system that modifies their behavior and responses to stimuli after lived experiences through neural synapses. This modification in neural circuits is called learning and it happens in the nervous system through a quality called **neural plasticity**. After each modification, we have an alteration in our beliefs and our results.

I will borrow a more complete definition of neural plasticity from Elenice Ferrari, researcher at the University of Campinas (Unicamp):

Neural plasticity is the brain's ability to develop new synaptic connections between the neurons through experience and behavior. With certain stimuli, there can be changes in the organization and localization of the information process in the brain. It is through plasticity that humans learn new behaviors and development becomes a continual act. The principle of this phenomenon is that the brain is not unchangeable, since neural plasticity allows for a determined function of the Central Nervous System (CNS) to be developed in another location in the brain as a result of learning and training.

You might be asking yourself: "What good are those technical terms? Why do I want to know what neural plasticity or neural network is?" The answer is simple: if your behavior and your lifestyle were learned, it means you can re-learn them. If you learned to be poor, you can learn to be rich—to think like a rich man, to feel like a rich man, and to make money like rich people.

It is possible you had a hard past that generated the learning of depressive behaviors, or neural circuits that promote a sad, meaningless life. The existence of neural plasticity means you are not doomed to be a sad, depressive person for the rest of your life. You can learn to be happy and lofty right now! Neural plasticity is equal to hope and freedom. It is like saying: "My life is fixable and I can be better and happier today."

My goal with this book is to produce enough emotional and cognitive stimuli for new neural synapses to happen; to provide a new, different way of connecting your neurons. And the best part is that those changes happen fast, very fast. I will show that to you now.

When I was a child, I had a bountiful, fun, joyous life in Rio de Janeiro. I was uninhibited, daring, and polite, taking into account the energy typical of a healthy 8-year-old. Around that time, the 1970s, I had quite *musical feet*, to the point that, at school parties, my friends' mothers used to choose me as their girls' dancing partner. Something happened, however, an experience that drastically changed my behavior and, consequently, my whole life. You might be imagining something tragic, devastating, catastrophic, but really, what happened to me was something that probably also happened to you, in different nuances.

Since I knew my mother got very proud when I was invited to be the *birthday girl's dancing partner*, I decided to go above and beyond during the 1975 Carnaval. At the time I was with my family at the Piraquê club, celebrating the holidays, and I decided to learn *carioca-style samba* and surprise my mom and dad. I saw a girl with a Carmen Miranda costume who could dance very well, so I started to imitate her. She saw it, and soon we became a duo like the Carnaval standard-bearers. She would *samba*, and I would imitate her. But remember, I had a goal with all that: to surprise my mom and dad dancing one more musical style—since my mom got so proud when I was asked to dance rock with my friends, just imagine if they also invited me to dance *samba*! (That was little Paulo's mind at 8, loving to meet his parents' expectations.)

After training a lot with my new partner, I figured I knew enough and would please my parents with my *samba*. I ran to the table they were sharing with another couple and enthusiastically yelled: "Dad, mom, I learned to *samba*." They looked skeptically at me and I started to frantically shake my hands and feet and move my whole body. After my over-the-top grand-finale, I looked at my parents and asked: "Do you like my *samba*, mom? Do you, dad?" My father coldly said one single sentence: "Completely out of tempo," and turned his back to me. Meanwhile, my mother tried to conceal the shame she felt for her clumsy son, and turned back to the table without saying anything, ignoring my presence. I vividly remember my parents' friends trying to pretend not to see my embarrassment.

Feeling completely alone and abandoned, with a major feeling of inadequacy after my first big rejection in life, I went back to the dance floor, this time to hide amidst the other children. And don't ask me what happened after that, because I don't remember anything else. This could go unnoticed or be unimportant, if not for the fact that that moment completely changed my behavior and attitude towards life: from that day on, I lost my tempo for dancing and singing. That wasn't all: even as a child, I started feeling panic of rejection or public ridicule and since then avoided all situations in which I could be exposed to it. And when the risk was imminent and inevitable, I myself assumed an uncoordinated, doltish—after all, it was easier to be rejected by myself than by other people.

I lived with these limiting beliefs until I was 30, when I began to learn to reprogram beliefs, starting with my own. When I reprogrammed my individual beliefs, all the communication potential that was buried in me surfaced. So, I became a teacher and speaker, breaking once and for all the blockage that for so long had kept me from doing what I wanted. With my example, I show it is not true when people say changes don't happen or take too long when they do. With thirty seconds of *samba* and ten seconds experiencing my parents' reaction, this new learning endured for a good part of my life.

If it still isn't clear that changes happen fast, I have another case, from one of my coaching clients to narrate to you. She was a beautiful regional manager in a pharmaceutical lab, where she was commercially responsible for three states. On a Monday morning, she got up, kissed her husband,

and said goodbye, since she would only be back next Wednesday. After the kisses and farewells, she went to the airport, only to discover one of the takeoff lanes was being renovated and the flight had been rescheduled without her knowledge.

She came back home, thrilled to be able to make a surprise breakfast for her husband and spend some more time with him, since her flight was only in the late afternoon. She tiptoed into the house and started to prepare breakfast when she heard voices coming from her bedroom. Getting close to the ajar door, she saw her husband and her best friend in the height of sexual climax. The emotional impact was so great she couldn't stand anymore and fell on her knees, looking astounded at the scene. When she opened the door, her husband jumped out of bed and went towards her, saying it wasn't what she thought and that he could explain it all. Baffled, astonished, and beside herself, she got up and left. She contacted her father and her two brothers, all lawyers, and immediately got divorced.

Time passed, the pain and disappointment dissipated, and life went back to normal. Soon, she was hired by another lab, with even better benefits. In less than a year, she had overcome the heartbreak and was once again strong and happy. However, something had changed drastically inside. When she hired me as her coach, the incident was four years in the past, and during all that time she hadn't gotten involved with any men, and her once intense and quality social life was down to just her parents, brothers, and a few male friends. At our first coaching session, I asked her what kept her from having relationships with other men, since she was young, beautiful, and successful.

Crying, she told me she didn't know. And added: "It's like I'm using a man repellent. I want to have a relationship, I want a boyfriend, I want to remarry and have a family, but I honestly don't know what makes men run from me. I know I'm pretty, nice, and successful, but nothing works. And the same thing happens with friendships. I invite someone out, but it's like there is no connection to maintain the relationship." When she finished her narrative, still in tears, she asked: "Can I be fixed?" Happily, with the help of CIS® Method and individual sessions of Integral Systemic Coaching with me, she reached a level of results even better than before the trauma. She improved not only conjugally but also in friendships. Today, she is married, has kids, and got promoted.

Once again, we witness a rapid, but traumatic experience that drastically changed someone's destiny. And when I say a drastic change of destiny, I don't mean the divorce, but the fact that a very pretty, very successful, very nice woman couldn't have friends or lovers anymore. The traumatic experience lasted just a few seconds, but was enough to change her beliefs about these interactions. So, I say again: beliefs determine behaviors and attitudes, and can change fast.

I will now explain in practice what are neural synapses, neural network, and neural plasticity. And this understanding, used in real life to change beliefs, was exactly what led me to teach in the United States and make Febracis a world reference in coaching.

Learning equals changing, and understanding is just knowing. The difference between these two things is what differentiates those who do from those who just think about doing.
(Paulo Vieira)

It is common knowledge that every stimulus produces neural synapses and if those same stimuli are received repeatedly or under heavy emotional impact they will produce new neural networks containing new beliefs, mental programming, or learnings (call it what you like). So, just one stimulus under heavy emotional impact, in the case of our beautiful pharmaceutical manager, was enough to change her internal programming about what marriage and friendship meant. In other words, what the manager saw (visual stimulus) and what she heard (auditory stimulus) under heavy emotional stress changed her beliefs about men and female friends. And, from that point on, even if unconsciously, she started to push away amorous relationships and friendships, especially female ones. The mental programming or learning resulting from that painful experience was: men (love partners) and friends are unreliable and will make me suffer; if I have them in my life, I will be hurt and disappointed, so I step away from them.

The same thing happened to me and samba. Seeing my father and mother turn their backs on me because of my clumsy dancing in front of so many friends was the painful visual stimulus. And the auditory stimulus was my father's line, full of reproach: "Completely out of tempo." These stimuli lasted a few seconds, but were enough to create a traumatic belief with the following programming: Run from any situation where you are exposed to mistake or ridicule, or you will be rejected.

Both me and that pharmaceutical manager started to live according to that programming, and every time we faced the stimulus in question the program was turned on and our behaviors were immediately, drastically altered. In my case, the change was explicit: everyone saw my inability to dance, to start a relationship with a girl, or my fear of making a mistake in soccer. It would be hard to list every situation I deprived myself of throughout my childhood, adolescence, and adulthood because of that mental programming or belief. For the pharmaceutical manager, changes were subtle; she didn't even realize her modified behavior, just experienced a lonely, needy life for four years.

These two might make it seem like new beliefs, neural plasticity, and changes that only bring negative consequences. This isn't true. It is very important for you to know that neural synapses happen with any stimulus, be it repeated or new. However, for new stimuli to create change, they need to be repeated many times or just once under heavy emotional impact—and only in this last case the change is fast. This, after all, is what happened to me that Carnaval, and to the manager.

To understand better the power of fixation and learning under heavy emotional impact, answer the following questions:

Where were you at 10 a.m. on October 3rd last year? You can't guess or assume; if you don't know, just write "I don't know."
Answer: _____

Now answer: Where were you at 10 a.m. on September 11th, 2001?
Answer: _____

If you are like most the world population (I have asked that question in four different continents), you will have remembered with little effort where you were and what you were doing on September 11th, 2001, but couldn't remember where you were just a year ago. This is because the human mind memorizes or learns better under heavy emotional impact. A stimulus that is not so important generates an electrical and chemical flow in the neurons, capable of producing few neural synapses; whereas a stimulus with strong emotional impact generates a gigantic electrical and chemical electrical charge, in which deep, strong learnings are stored, as well as a much broader memory of what has happened.

My challenge is to cause sensory stimuli (auditory, visual, and synesthetic) that is strong and repeated enough to produce new changes in people—along with the beliefs of a new life. I will say it again, so you don't lose perspective of our goal here: you can drastically and quickly change your marriage, your health and your physical appearance, your company, or your career. There is no limit to our possibilities other than self-imposed ones.

REALITY VERSUS IMAGINATION

There is one question left standing: how to cause a precise and specific sensory stimulus (visual, auditory, and synesthetic), capable of changing my limiting beliefs? How can I use impactful stimuli to reprogram my financial belief and end the financial limitations in which I live? How can I use these stimuli to cure my belief about impotence in the face of challenges, victimization, and depression, and to be happy in any situation? How can I use this strategy of reprogramming beliefs to reshape my body without losing quality of life in other areas?

To continue, you need to know that the human mind does not distinguish what is real from what is imagined. The human brain doesn't know the difference between a real experienced, lived in practice, and an experience that is just imagined. Encephalograms have offered proof of that a long time ago; today, however, with technological advancements, this finding is even more patent. One experiment is done using functional MRI and exposing the subject to a real stimulus, for instance, music. While they listen to the music, their synapses are mapped by the MRI equipment. Then, scientists turn off the music and ask for the volunteer to mentally sing the same song. What they realize is that the same areas of the brain are activated. The same experience was done with photographs; the brain area stimulated when the subject actually saw the photo was the same area stimulated when they just conceptualized it.

TO THE HUMAN BRAIN: REAL = IMAGINED

To sum up, our mind is the battle field. We don't need to go to Africa to kill a lion every day, neither to take part in a war in the Middle East. We don't need to get on the octagon to fight against MMA fighter Anderson Silva either. All this can happen in our minds, and the best part is that we can have control over what will happen and how. In the mind, experiences and stimuli not only are planned and under control, but are also much safer when correctly executed.

BELIEFS AS A THERMOSTAT

I will use the air-conditioner as a metaphor to explain belief programming. Let's assume you enter a room that is 86 °F, and the first thing you do is decide which temperature you want. You hold the control, point it to the machine, and program it to 71 °F. The air-conditioner sounds a "beep" to mean that the new temperature was programmed. Since the room was at 86 °F, the machine will make the ventilator work in full force, throwing cold air into the room and taking hot air out. Then, slowly, the temperature drops to 82 °F, 78 °F, 75 °F. When it gets to 70 °F, what happens? The machine's compressor stops cooling and obeys the previously programmed temperature, 71 °F, rising one degree. When it goes over 71 °F, the compressor automatically turns on and cools the room again, searching for the original 71 °F programming. And this happens endlessly, always according to the 71 °F programming marked in the remote control; sometimes a little over, sometimes a little under. To sum up, when the temperature goes over the programming, the equipment turns on and cools the environment, and the same is true for when it gets colder than programmed: the equipment turns off and lets the temperature rise, over and over again.

Like an air-conditioner, beliefs about marriage, financial life, professional success, health, and everything else are almost completely programmed since the end of puberty. Therefore, the tendency is for results to remain stable or very similar throughout life. This means poor people tend to remain poor, rich people, even if they lose their fortune, tend to get it back. The same way, happy people, even if they go through a painful event, tend to go back to being happy, while sad, melancholic people tend to stay like that even when everything is going well. As you know, everything is programmed. The problem is when this programming is dysfunctional and drives the person away from a pleasurable, full, abundant life.

Taking our financial life as an example, we are all programmed to keep having the financial pattern we learned in childhood, with the stimuli received during that time. Even people who have had a poor childhood and prosper usually carry their quota of behavior and attitudes of poorness inside them, keeping them from experiencing the fullness of their financial riches. Unlike the air-conditioning control, which you can reprogram at any time, we don't always know what beliefs are registered or programmed in our financial future. After all, how many young people are born rich, but lose everything in adulthood? How many people do you know who one day had it all and could do everything and in the other had nothing and couldn't do anything.

In one of my events, I met a man who was introduced to me as a very successful person, financially and professionally. During our talk, however, I detected non-verbal words and expressions typical of a poor, limited person. I questioned his sister in law, who was my personal friend, and alerted her that I had observed by his communication that he would certainly have serious financial trouble. She laughed, called her husband (the man's brother), and told him what I had said. He, in turn, very politely thanked my warning, but claimed everything was fine with his brother and that his business was running quite smoothly. The fact is that in October, just eight months later, that very successful businessman was completely broke and relying on family members to pay his most basic bills. If he had the awareness and tools to reprogram his financial beliefs, which even he didn't know he possessed, he certainly would have done that.

How about you, what beliefs and mental programming are ruling your life now and will determine your near future? We don't know the exact programming of our beliefs—if it is to stay married, to get divorced, or to have the best marriage in the world. That's the biggest risk for human beings, the unpredictability of our rooted beliefs. However, as you know, neural plasticity gives us the ability to change our beliefs at any time. You also know changes happen fast when we use the right neural mechanisms and strategies. So, I ask: what did you do with the information and exercises in the previous chapters? If you are awake, self-accountable, able to communicate with accuracy, focused, and inquiring; then, a good part (or most) of your beliefs are redone, and you can raise your head and dream about what is best inside and outside yourself.

SELF-ESTEEM

Simply put, self-esteem is how much a person wishes the best for herself. However, for you to wish the best for yourself, you need a combination of three beliefs that, together, make up an individual: the belief identity, which is about being (I am); the ability belief, which is about doing (I can or I am capable); and finally the merit belief, which is about having (I deserve).

BELIEF:	EMOTIONAL SKILL	BEHAVIOR / ATTITUDE
MERIT	I HAVE	HAVING
ABILITY	I CAN	DOING
IDENTITY	I AM	BEING

Let's analyze separately each of the beliefs that make up a person.

BELIEF IN BEING OR IDENTITY BELIEF

Looking at the pyramid, we can see the basis of the individual is in the identity belief. It is the identity belief that defines who you are and, obviously, your results. To understand how important identity belief is in someone's life and results, answer the questions below (it is very important that you answer it in writing using the lines below):

How do you relate to a dishonest person?
___

How do you treat a rude person?
___

How do you talk to a person who, in your opinion, is intellectually limited?
___

How much money would you lend someone who is unorganized and unsuccessful?
___

Would you give a job to a sad, miserable person, putting them with your current staff?
___

Would you marry a person with no values, adulterous, and promiscuous?

Would you be partners with a dishonest person?

Looking at your answers, it is clear the way you see yourself and those around. The answers also determine how you relate to them and treat them. If people are dishonest, you hold back and certainly don't share much information. If they are disorganized and confused, you probably won't give anything of yours for them to take care of, much less rely on them for tasks that require control and organization. If they are guilty, you will probably want justice and for them to pay for their mistakes. If they are worthless, you might not want to be connected to them; if they are promiscuous and adulterous, you might want total distance. If they are unimportant and dull, you might prefer to be with someone else, maybe someone more important and attractive.

What many people don't realize is that our perception of others determines our connection and relationship to them. Thus, our perception of ourselves, or our identity belief, determines our relationship to ourselves. The "I am" belief will determine whether or not I like myself. It will determine if I need to be rewarded or punished. It defines if I am going to win or lose. If I am going to have a relationship with a person of value or with someone worthless who will look down on me and abuse me. If I am going to cheat or be cheated. Your beliefs about yourself will determine everything from your self-value to your self-image, as well as all your results and behaviors.

A person certainly doesn't have just one identity belief, but a vast combination of identities that, together and combined in their proportions, make up the self. That is exactly why we use the term "individual," because there is only one person in the whole world with your combination of characteristics, generating a unique, exclusive potential. Believe me, there are things only you can do. When you in fact know who you are and, through self-questioning, find out your purpose and life mission, you will have an unbridled accomplishing power, and everything around you will conspire for you to do something grand.

OPPOSITES ATTRACT. DO THEY?

Lots of people don't understand how a beautiful, smart, successful, admirable woman can marry (or have a relationship with) a vulgar, worthless man. How many times have you seen that happen in a larger or smaller proportion, for example, a true womanizer having a relationship with a beautiful lady—like in a worsened version of *Lady and the Tramp*?

Those around the woman advise her, alert here, even beg for the relationship to end, saying she deserves better, that he is no good, she will suffer, this relationship can never work, and so on. But there is something in him that attracts her and draws her to this relationship. This is called homophily, man's natural tendency to relate to people who are like them. "What do you mean, 'who are like them?'," you might ask, after all, she is beautiful, cult, intelligent, admirable, and wanted by people around her, while he is a vulgar, worthless man, a womanizer. Homophily happens not only with observable similarities, but also internal ones, such as emotions and self-images. That woman sees in her exterior all that everyone else sees, but in the inside, her identity belief is just like his, or he complements hers. After all, a worthless woman will have a relationship with a worthless man or one who abuses her and doesn't cherish her.

I had a client come to me because he was involved with a hooker and couldn't get rid of the relationship. Intellectually, he knew the involvement was deprived, as he went every night to the whorehouse to wait for his lover to finish receiving her numerous clients. After all, a project engineer, two beautiful children, a gorgeous wife pregnant with their third child, and a prosperous company didn't match that lifestyle. But inside him, his identity brought him to that relationship pattern.

It all became clear when I found out the story of his childhood: raised with severe physical and moral punishments, he was always demeaned and compared to brothers, neighbors, acquaintances, strangers, and so on. They were all better than him, regardless of what he did; he was never good enough. And, as we know, everything he saw, heard, and felt from childhood until puberty defined his identity belief. The result of how he was raised and the beliefs it produced was that he was chained and stuck to someone very similar to him, in internal emotional aspects, not very tangible. In this case, it was amazing to see a new person rising, considering that man who was stuck in a worthless extramarital affair wasn't truly him. As a result of his new identity belief, he went back home to his marriage and his children, and his company close an exclusive deal with the three main construction companies in town.

Be that as it may, once again we see the power of the identity belief defining an individual's life and results. But don't worry: there are tools and mechanisms to reprogram those limiting beliefs. If everything we lived in our past was learned—and if part of that wasn't good—, we can, regardless of age, program new beliefs, extraordinary beliefs about who we are.

If someone has convinced you that you were a lazy punk, you can un-learn that. If the stimuli you got as a child said you were incapable of this or that, remember it was a learning and, if you learned that, you can re-learn new things about yourself. Neural plasticity and change in beliefs exist, new neural synapses can be made to create a new, deep neural network of who you are.

No one in my family could believe that at the age of 30, with a shattered life in every area—no money, broken business, abandoned by the first wife, no health, living and eating of goodwill in relatives' houses—, I could turn around and become an internationally renowned lecturer and coach, writer of many successful books. And they couldn't see me as a successful man, because I didn't see myself as such before I was 30. People act and react to you according to your identity belief. So, turn to yourself and rebuild what needs rebuilding.

BELIEF IN DOING OR ABILITY BELIEF

The ability to belief is determined by what you believe you are capable of doing or learning to do. This is the belief structure that will dictates your *potential* for accomplishment. However, as stated before, it only dictates the potential, for the accomplishment itself is determined by the combination of identity belief and ability belief.

To explain better, I will tell you the case of a coaching client of mine from years ago, who was very intelligent and had an enviable CV, whose lowest grade in all of Law School was a B. She was an organized, meticulous professional, and met every deadline, but didn't consider herself capable of facing another lawyer during a court hearing. So, she always tried to settle, which wasn't always ideal for her clients. She looked for impenetrable legal theses, found flawless jurisprudence, and was always ready to win, but never felt capable of going into direct confrontation with other lawyers or being confronted by a judge. This made it possible for her to help three of her lawyer colleagues, who became partners at the firm. She, on the other hand, who became famous for being the one with the potential, but not as the most capable one in terms of confrontation, ended up as audience to each of the inauguration ceremonies of the three partners she helped.

This case makes it clear that identity belief is not enough to ensure professional success. It wasn't enough for my client to see herself as a smart, valuable, honest, dedicated, committed person. She also needed to develop the belief in her ability to speak publicly, face other lawyers, and plead the sentences she defended before a judge. During the coaching process, I directed my work towards reprogramming specific ability beliefs she needed. She quickly started to face direct confrontations she had learned to avoid since childhood. By the way, she became partner in the same firm she worked, only five months after we started our coaching process.

BELIEF IN HAVING OR MERIT BELIEF

The third and last level is about having, that is, the merit belief that occupies the top of the pyramid that makes up an individual. My studies confirm that when we have a strong, adequate identity belief, aligned with an ability belief, we naturally start building a merit belief. It is true that the basis of our merit was programmed when we were still children, by means of the treatment and experiences received from our father and mother, or substitute parents. The same happens to our identity and ability beliefs.

People with low level of merit have a terrible self-sabotage addiction. After all, why would they have good experiences if inside them there is a belief that they don't deserve that much? This way, every time their life improves, they stumble on a maximum limit of merit and, then, display sabotaging behaviors, actions, or attitudes, and the gains and conquests go under. When these people with such a low level of merit get something good, they say: "You didn't deserve it." When someone compliments them, they say: "No, it's your eyes."

For most people, it is hard even to get a simple compliment, however, it's even harder to experience great victories. This learned thought that we don't deserve good things is limiting, like a low ceiling that keeps us from lifting up our head in our own house. It makes a person try to prosper and, after starting to have any type of success, hit their head on the ceiling and start to sabotage themselves. They lose their job, destroy their marriage with their own hands, break their company, then start all over again.

Do you know anyone who starts to have success in some area of life and soon sabotages themselves, loses what was won or conquered, and restarts a new battle to reconquer, and then lives it all again?

The three greatest characteristics of someone with a non-merit belief are: losing, not finishing what they started, and then restarting.
(Paulo Vieira)

Some people have success in one area of life and believe they are prosperous and deserving. Yes, they are prosperous and deserving in that specific area, but there are other areas that define and complement who we are. I am rich, but am I happy? I am healthy, but am I successful? Looking at it that way, a person may have achieved a wonderful marriage but has a lousy health. Another may have multiple assets, but a misfit family. Therefore, the non-merit belief can either be generalized and affect every area of someone's life or only impact one specific area or another.

My ideal wish is obviously to build a merit belief in every area of your life. You must be asking: "But how?"

I'll show you!

CHILDISH BELIEFS: HOW TO BUILD AND REBUILD THEM

Andrei, a 12-year-old boy, was found running naked in a remote area of Siberia, in 2004, where the temperature gets as low as -40 °F. Victor was found by hunters in the forest of Aveyron, in France, with 23 bite scars in his body. The girls Kamala, 8, and Amala, 1.5 year old, were found in a forest in India, in 1920. What do the stories of Andrei Tolstyk, Victor of Aveyron, and Kamala and Amala have in common? All four lived in total human isolation and were adopted and raised by wild animals from very early on, most of them before the age of 2.

They all displayed wild behavior, trotted and walked on arms and legs like four-legged animals; sniffed everything they ate; gnawed food, ate raw meat, roots, and fruits; didn't wear clothes; and didn't talk, only emitting guttural sounds. The girls died one year after leaving the jungle because they couldn't adapt to civilization. The Russian wolf-boy ran away; the suspicion is that environmentalists took him back to the cold mountains of Siberia before he died or became an object of research. And Victor of Aveyron died at 40 without having socialized or created human social bonds. And these aren't the only proven cases of children raised by animals. There are dozens in the literature, always with the same result: children or teenagers who live like perfect animals in the woods and don't have any conditions to adapt to human social standards.

I mention the wild children here to make it clear that our human side—emotions, sociability, behaviors, moral, ethics, values—as well as everything a person is and can be and do, come from learning with all they see, hear, and especially feel throughout childhood. This means that parents and home environment are what make all the difference in the child's future life. In this perspective, it is common to hear: "Aren't other environments, like the school and the neighborhood, important?" Yes, they are, but these environments are just a reflection of the parents' belief in the context of who they are, what they can do and what they have (being, doing, and having). Essentially, parents who are emotionally skilled to educate their children will raise capable, victorious children, no matter where they live. And if the parents are or live in a chaotic environment, it is because their beliefs have attracted them there or produced the chaos.

The near totality of what wild children experienced was a wild way of communicating, thinking, and feeling. Based on the stimuli they received, the only belief system they learned was how to feed themselves and survive in the jungle like their peers, adoptive parents, and teachers: the beasts. What I will analyze from now on is how domestic stimuli can produce both bountiful, happy, socially harmonic humans or literate, unhappy, scarce, socially misfit animals.

In 1998, a study involving over 17,000 people (almost all from the middle class with good financial conditions), was conducted and led by a multidisciplinary team made up of doctors Vince Felitti and Bob Anda, of the United States Center for Disease Control (CDC), and followed by 57 papers until 2011, broadly divulged by doctor Nadine Burke[1] . This study showed that the witnessing of all the following situations: physical abuse, sexual abuse, moral and emotional harassment, care and affection negligence, violence by family members, abandonment, discord at home, parents' divorce, family members' chemical addictions and its consequences, can produce overwhelming damages on children, and from very early ages. And the results will accompany people throughout their adult lives, until they can reprogram their beliefs and diminish or undo the effects of Adverse Childhood Experiences (ACEs).

There are three types of damages caused by ACEs that manifest very early and will resonate through adult life:

1º) Physical problems and illnesses.
2º) Emotional problems and illnesses.
3º) Social and behavioral problems.

---

[1] Nadine Burke Harris is a pediatrician, founder and CEO of the Center for Youth Wellness.

In lectures about this research, doctor Nadine shows that seven out of ten deaths in the Western world are caused by ACEs. And it doesn't stop there. She demonstrates, with a lot of research, that the more adversity episodes in the childhood, the more deficient the immune system will be throughout life, leaving people susceptible to the simplest flu or infection. Studies also confirm her pediatric practice, with episodes of ACE affecting the human hormonal system, causing various diseases and endocrine dysfunctions. With the researches' advancement, we saw that ACEs more than triple the chances of a stroke or heart attack. And when they thought they had discovered everything that affected people who underwent these episodes, they still discovered that children exposed to varied, constant ACE have three times more chance of having cancer than someone with less episodes. Children who have been exposed to varied and frequent ACEs were twelve times more likely to commit suicide. All this not to mention tripled disposition for drug use and smoking, as well as delinquency, crime, and social maladjustment.

There is a simple neuroscientific explanation: when a child is exposed to a real or imaginary risk, their hypothalamus sends a signal to the pituitary gland, which, in turn, stimulates the adrenal gland. The last releases adrenaline and cortisol. Thus, this small child is ready to *flight or figh*t the wolf that threatens her. With these molecules of emotion, the child will have stronger heart beats pumping blood to the extremities, for strength and muscle explosion. She will also have heightened reflexes, and feel less pain in case of a strike.

This chemical transformation would be much needed if this child was having to face other animals in the forest. The dysfunctional learning that made the child addicted and chemically dependent on the molecules of emotion that combine adrenaline and cortisol to low levels of serotonin and endorphin was a dangerous wolf (threat) coming to their home every night, so the choices were to flee, freeze, or attack. What should be an evolutionary adaptation to face a threat was repeated so many times during this child's infancy that it stopped being an adaptation for threat and became an addiction to adversity itself and its molecules of emotion.

Children are especially sensitive to adverse traumatic experiences, not only because their brain is in formation, but because neural plasticity is much easier and more present until the age of 12. And these molecules of emotion, good or bad, will become the child's future addictions or virtues. Since they saw, heard, and felt those experiences, it will be easy for them to reproduce these environments, circumstances and molecules of emotion as adults.

These ACEs not only alter and harm the adult's brain but also affect immune system, hormonal system, and alter DNA structure, activating or not a given chromosome through genetic triggers.

ACE QUIZ

There are ten types of childhood trauma measure in the ACE study. Five are personal—physical abuse, verbal abuse, sexual abuse, physical negligence, emotional negligence—, and the other five are connected to other members of the family—an alcoholic father, a mother victim of domestic violence, a relative in jail, a relative diagnosed with a mental illness, and the disappearance of a parent due to divorce, death, or abandonment. Each trauma counts as one point. So, a person who was physically abused, with an alcoholic father, and a mother who was beaten has an ACE score of three.

There are, obviously, many other types of trauma—witnessing a sibling being abused, losing a caregiver (grandmother, mother, grandfather etc.), homelessness, surviving and recovering from a severe accident, witnessing a father being abused by a mother, witnessing a grandmother abusing a father, and so on. The ACE study included only the ones aforementioned because they were cited as the most common by a group of about 300 people in an American psychology clinic. These traumas were also individually studied in scientific literature.

The most important thing to remember is that ACE score is a guideline: If you have experienced other types of toxic stress over months or years, this will increase your risk of health consequences.

Answer the questions below from the Adverse Childhood Experience quiz with "yes" or "no" and find out your possible results.

Before your 18th birthday:

1.	Did a parent or other adult in the household often or very often swear at you, insult you, humiliate you, or act in a way that made you afraid you might be physically hurt? _____
2.	Did a parent or other adult in the household often or very often push, grab, slap, throw something or hit you so hard you had marks or injuries? _____
3.	Did a parent or person at least five years older than you ever touch or fondle you or have you touch their body in a sexual way or attempt or actually have intercourse with you? _____
4.	Did you often or very often feel that no one in your family loved you or thought you were important or special? Or your family didn't look out for each other, feel close to each other, or support each other? _____
5.	Did you often have little or very little to eat and no one to protect you? Did you often have to wear dirty clothes? Were your parents too drunk or too high to take care of you or to take you to the doctor if you needed it? _____
6.	Was a biological parent ever lost to you through divorce, abandonment, or other reason? _____
7.	Was your mother or stepmother often or very often pushed, grabbed, slapped, or had something thrown at her? Or was this person at some time kicked, bitten, hit with a fist? Was she hit in any other way or threatened with a gun or knife? _____
8.	Did you live with anyone who was a problem drinker or alcoholic, or who used street drugs? _____
9.	Was a household member depressed or mentally ill, or did a household member attempt suicide? _____
10.	Did a household member go to prison _____
Each "yes" is equivalent to 1 point. Add your tally: ____. This is your ACE score.

As your ACE score increases, so does your risk for illness, social and emotional problems. With an ACE score equal to or higher than 4, negative results throughout life start to get more critical. The probability of chronic pulmonary disease increases 390%; hepatitis, 240%; depression, 460%; suicide, 1,220%.

It is very important to take into account that the research about adversities experienced during childhood involved 17,000 people who weren't poor, unschooled, or lived in the outskirts. On the contrary, it was done with people with good university education and good jobs. This means even people who are apparently well-adjusted and successful suffer from emotional, health, and behavioral problems if they have undergone adverse experiences as children. This is clear in the graphs below:

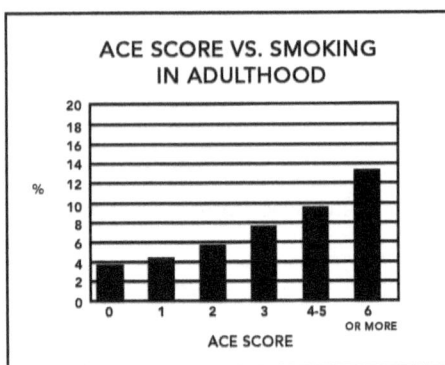
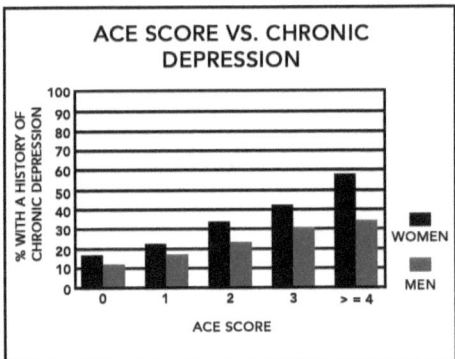
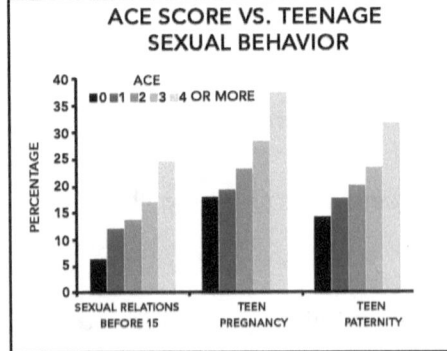
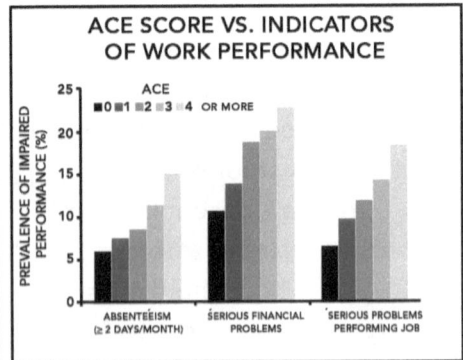

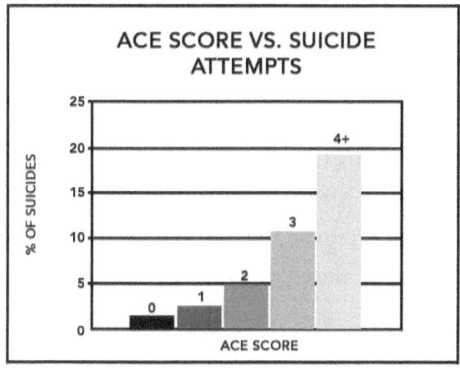 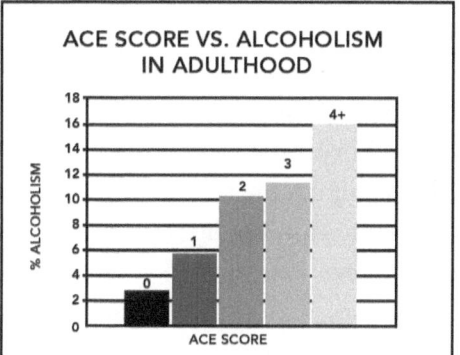

Source of graphs: <http://acestoohigh.com/got-your-ace-score/>.

If you still weren't convinced that visual, auditory, and sensory stimuli communicated during childhood shape our beliefs, lives, and results in every aspect, this should now be clearer. What type of communication did you experience as a child? Communication of love, lack of love, or anger? I can ask the same thing in another way: How many ACEs did you have until you were 18? Looking at your life and results and connecting it with the graphs above, how much effort does it take to rewrite your beliefs and not be a part of ACE statistics? It doesn't matter how many points you got in the quiz, what matters is what you will do about it.

The CIS® Method, the Systemic Integral Coaching Training, individual coaching sessions, and this book are strategies to help you recreate your beliefs. There is no shortage of tools. As you saw in the testimonies in the beginning of the book, it is all real, and big changes are possible. You can and will change your life and feel much better. However, it is still up to you to act and do what needs to be done.

THE BEGINNING OF CHANGE

Considering the beliefs of being, doing, and having are so interdependent and interconnected, every time you enhance one, the others improve along. But, as we have seen, there is a natural order that starts with "being."

Then, as a result of who I am, I start "doing" things. Finally, when I am who I am and do what I do, the logical, natural consequence is to have the things that correspond to that.

Unfortunately, however, a good part of humanity is still lost searching for fleeting, ephemeral things to make them feel better about themselves. Consumption media has been inducing many people who don't question themselves to invert the pyramid and, thus, also subvert their personal values, behaviors, and goals. Our society is looking first at the "have" part: I have money, I have a big car, I have luxury clothes, I have expensive watches, etc. In reality, when we try the "having" before the "being" approach we want to compensate for the fragile, deficient way we see and believe ourselves to be in our essence. After all, if I have a big car, people will see me differently, and say that "I am rich, successful, intelligent". If I see my bank account as being full and more bountiful than those of the people around me, I will feel better, richer, more renowned and more important. And who knows, maybe my self-image won't bother me that much. So, ostentation becomes my motto. A popular saying describes ostentation as: "Buying what I don't need with money I don't have to show to those I don't like the person I want to be."

For a year, I did volunteer work in a prison, and my interviews with inmates showed me why the overwhelming majority started a life in crime. The only reason they gave was that they wanted or needed to "have" something. However, when I went deeper in the interviews, it wasn't just the desire to "have" that led them on that path, for before they wanted to "have," their identity beliefs had been completely disfigured by all types of childhood problems, traumas, and pain, like: sexual abuse, domestic violence, physical aggression, addicted parents, orphanage, abandonment, and every other kind of emotional pain. So, behind the image of a delinquent young man there is the self-image of a thief, murderer, robber, rapist, drug dealer. Don't think those people are imprisoned or doing crime on the outside just because they want to have something. If that were the case, you and I would right now be killing or stealing to "have" our dreams. And if we are not, it is for two reasons: fear of the consequences or because that doesn't match who we are.

So, the inmates were doing crime because their identity beliefs, the way they saw themselves, had been altered. I want to take this opportunity to alert governments and everyone who works with ex-prisoners: don't think that just working on their ability belief, and teaching them a job, will in fact reintegrate them in society. Even if they do learn a profession, what will determine their behavior and attitude will still be their identity belief. And if they keep seeing themselves as a worthless, cruel, violent, hateful victim of society, they will have a new job, but still see themselves as a lowlife. Besides teaching a profession and working on "doing," the judiciary system and organizations engaged with the cause also need to work on recreating these people's identity belief, that is, their "being." For when they see themselves as citizens, not thugs; when they see themselves as good people, not evil; when they see themselves as valiant, not unsolvable criminals, then they will be able to live side by side with you or me, without relapsing and going back to jail.

I need to do an aside to congratulate all the Christian churches with which I had contact over that year of volunteering in detention, because they did just that: worked on identity beliefs. How? Through constant preaching, Bible readings, hymns and songs of praise to God. With continuous evangelistic stimuli, the inmates started to see themselves as God's children, as the image and likeness of God. And a passage from the Bible they constantly cited to me was the one that said they were like clay in the potter's hands, remade and with their pasts erased. They were now new creatures.

I met a young woman who was going to marry a very wealthy man, but loved another. And I asked her: "Why are you marrying someone you don't love?" To which she answered: "He can give me everything I never had." I added: "It's true, he can give you everything, including misery." I went on to question: "Is what he has more important to you than who he is?" I asked a lot of powerful questions, but she and her mother were convinced this was the best alternative.

Why did that young woman make a decision like that? Simple, because it didn't matter to her who she was, but what she would "have." You can imagine how this marriage ended: in divorce, after the husband caught her in a motel with her ex-boyfriend who was the love of her life. And for her complete frustration, she came out of the marriage with no money at all. To make it all worse, the ex-boyfriend didn't want her either after what happened. After all, he couldn't give her what she wanted.

One woman came to me at one of my seminars to say thank you, saying she had been watching my videos online since April, and that alone had made her quit being a luxury prostitute. At that time, she had decided to leave her flat, sell her car to pay for college, and move back with her parents. When I asked why she had made that decision, she answered: "I'm tired of having clothes, jewelry, cars, and luxury trips. What I want for myself right now is to be someone worthy. Someone my parents and I can be proud of. I'll go back home, start college again, graduate, and be happy."

I would like to tell you the story of a businessman who was once the richest in a given country. I cite him as an example of an inversion of being, doing, and having. One night, I watched an interview he gave to a TV show. In that talk, he told the reporter he wanted to be the richest man in the world, so he would be respected. At the time, I mumbled to the TV, as if he could hear me: "If what you want is respect, you're going about it in the wrong way." Sometime later, that man had his assets and personal items confiscated for auctions, after being accused of manipulating the market and inside trading. Now, his name and his companies are a joke all over the world. All this in the name of "having," for he believed that if he had the largest patrimony in the world, then he would be (being) respected. As we know, he first needed to "be" a super-businessman and, when his competence became clear and patent through his business actions (doing), then, as a consequence, he could "have" the largest fortune in the world.

These are the three possible results for those who invert the natural order of the individual:

1°) Having, but becoming unhappy.
2°) Never having, living in an unbridled, exhausting search.
3°) Having, getting to the top of the merit pyramid, and harshly falling.

Now, let's understand and investigate which your beliefs and values are about the three formative beliefs are. Get your notebook and answer the following PWQs honestly:

POWERFUL WISDOM QUESTIONS:

What calls your attention the most to people around you: what they are, what they can do, or what they have? List three people you admire and describe each in what they are most successful: Being, doing, or having.
_____
_____
_____

What is best about you? Who you are as a human being, what you do professionally, or what you have?
_____
_____

When was the last time you looked for something to have to feel better or more important?
_____
_____

How much do you do for everyone around you to be more valued and loved by them?
_____
_____

Are drinking or smoking ways of doing something to feel more accepted, more important, or more powerful?
_____
_____
_____

What are your twenty best personal characteristics as far as being?
___
___
___

What are the seven main things you can do that make you feel the proudest?
___
___

What do you try the hardest to show people: what you have, what you do, or who you are?
___
___

Looking at the individual pyramid adjacent, what percentage do you attribute to each of the three areas considering the importance you have been giving to each in your way of living?

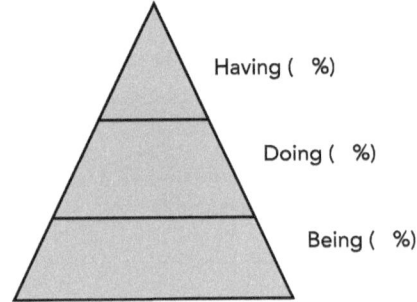

Having (%)

Doing (%)

Being (%)

Is the importance you give people based on who they are as human beings, what they do—their job, business position, type of work, etc.—or the money and patrimony they own? Fill it in the individual pyramid.

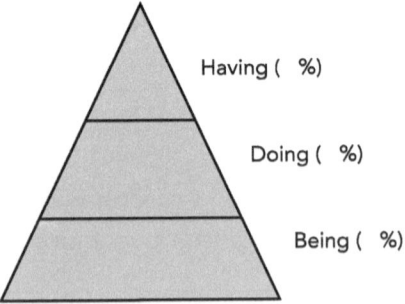

Having (%)

Doing (%)

Being (%)

A great way of remaking your self-esteem is putting the individual pyramid in the right order, recreating your lifestyle and prioritizing your positive personal characteristics. Then, take advantage of those personal attributes and do the best they allow you to do in each area of life. Therefore, you will finally **have** everything your **being** allowed you to **do**.

Final Message

You have awoken. Before reading this book you might have been asleep for life and possibilities, but now you are awake. That is what matters. Awake, you act, you do the right thing, you do your best. Only those who act have power, and you know that. In every action, every look, you direct your focus. Changes happen when you have focus.

Position your focus on a timeline and direct it towards the future, for that is where time runs, but act in the present, today. Plan to act. Power is in action, especially the right action. This way, I am sure your life will be extraordinary, abundant, prosperous, and happy. There will be prosperity in big and small things. Even the worst afflictions can and should create learnings and more abundance in your existence. After all, with every storm we build a stronger ship.

You have awakened, acted, and focused. So, communicate the perfect language of God's love. Communicate the best possible things with your eyes, your semblance and your posture. The desire to communicate bad things will come, but now you are awake and, thus, know how to act and how to make a difference. The important thing isn't what happens, but what I do with what happens. You are free to act and be the captain of your ship. You are the author of your life's book. Remember, you are the only one capable of change. You are where you put yourself. What happens to you is completely your merit, be it because of your actions—conscious or unconscious—, the quality of your thoughts, your behaviors, or your words. You put your life where it is now, therefore, only you can change it.

Everything is going well, but realize it can still get better. It is enough to question what happened and what can still happen. Think about what you did, what you will do, and what you can do better. What is special about great world thinkers is not their I.Q., but the fact that they are constantly questioning themselves. Leonardo da Vinci examined everything around. He questioned himself about anatomy, dissected the human body, and understood every muscle we know. Da Vinci didn't know how the human body worked and, from there, decided to question the how and why of everything around him. Why not question? Why not recreate your thoughts about the world today? You can be sure that it will make a positive difference to you and those around you. Questioning is very lucky!

You have awakened to life. You communicate better and act more assertively. Ask yourself about what you can still change about yourself. That is how we wake up to be more. And why not? After this process, you believe the best and understand how beliefs work. You recreated your beliefs, you know you are capable and deserve the best. After reading these pages, you have awakened and become a better parent, child, sibling, professional and person. You have an abundant lifestyle. You are already eliminating your traumatic beliefs. Enjoy this moment we call present, because something grand is already happening inside you!

So, welcome to your new life. Wake up. Communicate. Focus. The best is yet to come! The best starts now, at the end of this book, the moment you put everything you learn into practice. That is the only way to have a really extraordinary life. We were conceived for victory and success. We have the ability to make a better world and leave positive marks for future generations. Live this extraordinary life and communicate it to everyone around you. Everyone can be better than they are. You are now a beacon of possibilities not only for yourself, but for other people too.

Love, affection, and respect,

Paulo Vieira

REFERENCES

ANDREAS, Steve; FAULKNER, Charles; COMPREHENSIVE, Equipe de Treinamento da Nlp. *PNL: A nova tecnologia do sucesso.* Rio de Janeiro: Campus, 2003. 319 p.

ARNTZ, William. *Quem somos nós?* Rio de Janeiro: Prestigio, 2007. 276 p.

ARORA, Harbans Lal. *Terapias quânticas*: cuidando do ser inteiro. Rio de Janeiro: Qualitymark, 2008. 288 p.

BANDLER, Richard. *Usando sua mente:* as coisas que você não sabe que não sabe. 7. ed. São Paulo: Summus, 1987. 184 p.

BANDLER, Richard; GRINDER, John. *A estrutura da magia:* um livro sobre linguagem e terapia. São Paulo: Guanabara, 2012. 272 p.

BRADBERRY, Travis; GREAVES, Jean. *Emotional intelligence 2.0.* San Diego: Talentsmart, 2009. 192 p.

BRANDEN, Nathaniel. *Autoestima e os seus seis pilares.* São Paulo: Saraiva, 1998. 398 p.

BROWN, Jeff; FENSKE, Mark; NEPORENT, Liz. *O cérebro do vencedor:* 8 táticas científicas para você alcançar o sucesso. Rio de Janeiro: Elsevier, 2010. 216 p.

CARSON, Shelley. *O cérebro criativo.* Rio de Janeiro: Best Seller, 2012. 368 p.

CHAMINE, Shirzad. *Inteligência positiva:* por que só 20% das equipes e dos indivíduos alcançam seu verdadeiro potencial e como você pode alcançar o seu. Rio de Janeiro: Objetiva, 2013. 216 p.

CHRISTAKIS, Nicholas; FOWLER, James. *O poder das conexões.* Rio de Janeiro: Campus, 2009. 336 p.

DELL'ISOLA, Alberto. *Mentes brilhantes:* como desenvolver todo o potencial do seu cérebro. São Paulo: Universo dos Livros, 2012. 208 p.

EKMAN, Paul. *A linguagem das emoções.* São Paulo: Leya Brasil, 2011. 288 p.

EMMONS, Robert A. *Agradeça e seja feliz!* Rio de Janeiro: Best Seller, 2009. 304 p.

FLIPPEN, Flip; WHITE, Chris J. *Pare de se sabotar e dê a volta por cima.* Rio de Janeiro: Sextante, 2011. 224 p.

GARDENSWARTZ, Glee; ROWE, Anita; CHERBOSQUE, Jorge. *Inteligência emocional na gestão de resultados.* São Paulo: Clio, 2012. 232 p.

GEROMEL, Ricardo. *Bilionários:* o que eles têm em comum além de nove zeros antes da vírgula. São Paulo: Leya, 2014. 272 p.

GOLEMAN, Daniel. *Foco:* a atenção e seu papel fundamental para o sucesso. 1. ed. Rio de Janeiro: Objetiva, 2013. 296 p.

_____. *O poder da inteligência emocional.* Rio de Janeiro: Campus/Elsevier, 2002. 319 p.

GOSSETT, Don. *Há poder em declarar a Palavra de Deus.* Belo Horizonte: Atos, 2008. 256 p.

GRANT, Adam. *Dar e receber:* uma abordagem revolucionária sobre o sucesso, generosidade e influência. Rio de Janeiro: Sextante, 2014. 288 p.

HARRIS, Rachel Nolte; LAW, Dorothy. *As crianças aprendem o que vivenciam.* Rio de Janeiro: Sextante, 2009. 144 p.

LEADER, Darian; CORFIELD, David. *Por que as pessoas ficam doentes?* Rio de Janeiro: Best Seller, 2009. 336 p.

LIVINGSTONE, Bob. *A cura integrada de corpo, mente e alma:* livre-se das dores emocionais. São Paulo: Larousse, 2008. 160 p.

MAKTOUM, Hh Sheikh Mohammed Bin Rashid Al. *My vision:* challenges in the race for excellence. Dubai: Motivate Publishing, 2012. 214 p.

MARTIN, Steve J.; GOLDSTEIN, Noah; CIALDINI, Robert. *The small BIG:* small changes that spark big influence. Nova York: Grand Central Publishing, 2014. 288 p.

PAPASAN, Jay; KELLER, Gary. *A única coisa:* o foco pode trazer resultados extraordinários para sua vida. São Paulo: Novo Século, 2014. 208 p.

SELIGMAN, Martin E. P. *Aprenda a ser otimista.* 2 ed. Rio de Janeiro: Nova Era. 2005. 392 p.

SERVAN-SCHREIBER, David. *O stress, a ansiedade e a depressão sem medicamento nem psicanálise.* São Paulo: Sá Editora, 2004. 304 p.

TAYLOR, Jill Bolte. *A cientista que curou seu próprio cérebro.* Rio de Janeiro: Ediouro, 2008. 224 p.

TOLLE, Eckhart. *O despertar de uma nova consciência.* Rio de Janeiro: Sextante, 2007. 272 p.

VARELLA, Drauzio. "Estresse e depressão." Disponível em: <http://drauziovarella.com.br/drauzio/estresse-e-depressao/>. Acesso em: 5 mai. 2015.

WHITE, Ellen G.W. *Mente, caráter e personalidade.* São Paulo: Casa Publicadora Brasileira, 1996. 262 p.

DEAR READER,
We'd like to know your opinion about our books. After reading, follow our LinkedIn at linkedin.com/company/editora-gente, our TikTok and Instagram @editoragente, and visit our website at www.editoragente.com.br. Register to send suggestions, criticisms, or compliments. *Happy reading!*

**This book was printed
in B&W on 50lb
creme paper.**

www.ingramcontent.com/pod-product-compliance
Lightning Source LLC
LaVergne TN
LVHW090035080526
838202LV00044B/3330